The
Puppy No One
Wanted

Books by

BARBY KEEL

GABBY
The Little Dog That Had to Learn to Bark

WILL YOU LOVE ME?
The Rescue Dog That Rescued Me

THE PUPPY NO ONE WANTED
The Little Dog Desperate for a Home to Call His Own

Published by Kensington Publishing Corp.

The Puppy No One Wanted

The Little Dog
Desperate for a
Home to Call
His Own

BARBY KEEL

with Cathryn Kemp

CITADEL PRESS

Kensington Publishing Corp.

www.kensingtonbooks.com

CITADEL PRESS BOOKS are published by

Kensington Publishing Corp.
119 West 40th Street
New York, NY 10018

First published in Great Britain by Trapeze, an imprint of The Orion Publishing Group Ltd.

All Kensington titles, imprints, and distributed lines are available at special quantity discounts for bulk purchases for sales promotions, premiums, fund-raising, educational, or institutional use.

Special book excerpts or customized printings can also be created to fit specific needs. For details, write or phone the office of the Kensington sales manager: Kensington Publishing Corp., 119 West 40th Street, New York, NY 10018, attn: Sales Department; phone 1-800-221-2647.

ISBN-13: 978-0-8065-4114-3
ISBN-10: 0-8065-4114-8

First printing: July 2021

10 9 8 7 6 5 4 3 2 1

Printed in the United States of America

Electronic edition:

ISBN-13: 978-0-8065-4115-0 (e-book)
ISBN-10: 0-8065-4115-6 (e-book)

To Teddy

To the most wonderful dog in the world.
I'll always love you
and will see you again on Rainbow Bridge.

Barby x x x

CONTENTS

Introduction

Every fence, every gate, every inch of every acre of beautiful Sussex countryside that makes up the Barby Keel Animal Sanctuary has been built from nothing. There was never meant to be a rescue shelter on this land, and it is still one of the few remaining private sanctuaries in Britain, which is more a testament to my sheer bloody-mindedness than anything else. I have loved animals passionately since I was old enough to sit at my father's knee and watch him dole out love and care to the many wounded, stray and abandoned creatures he'd rescue on a daily basis. I grew up in small, rented terraced houses in Eastbourne, not the most likely of places to keep neglected creatures, but that fact didn't stop my father. A slight, unassuming man with a soft heart and the kindest face you've ever seen, my dad would buy up any animal that looked lonely or bedraggled from the local pet shops. He had an uncanny ability to attract any strays on the streets as well. I swear Dad was like the Pied Piper of animals. The sick, injured or lost would seek him out and he'd welcome them into our home. They'd follow him home, and more often than not, he would bring them inside, risking the severe wrath of my belligerent mother, and shower them with love and attention.

I loved the animals as much as my dad. I would amble in after school, always fearful of my mother's reaction at seeing me as I was always told off for being too dirty, too scruffy or having a scowl on my face. Yet the sight of the hamsters we kept in a makeshift cage, or the rabbit in the tiny garden out back, or the litter of kittens crawling and mewing over each other in a large cardboard box in the lounge, always filled me with happiness.

I recall one mongrel with black fur and a limp that Dad brought home one day. The mongrel had followed him home, and it was clear that the dog was injured. As always, my mother stood at the door protesting, but Dad would always, always stand firm. That dog limped into our house and into my heart, just like all the others that preceded and followed him. We called him Hop-a-Long, and Dad took him under his wing. He fetched some leftover sausages and fed them to him, gently stroking him until he found the wounded limb. When the young dog, which must only have been about a year old, winced, Dad shushed him and continued to stroke him, speaking so gently to it that it could've been a newborn baby.

I sat beside him as he treated the injured animal, watching the exchange in awe. Observing my father was how I learned to love, and he taught me how to be gentle and kind. I didn't learn that from my mother, for whom I could do nothing right. No, watching Dad was my passage to the knowledge of how caring for animals is ultimately an act of self-care for ourselves. I have always been fascinated by the exchange that happens between man and beast, carer and animal, for it isn't just the animal that is healed and comforted, but the person as well. The relationship between humans and animals is an ancient one, which lies beyond words. It is an endless cycle of mutual respect, a bond that reaches into our prehistoric past, and yet one I see acted out on my land every day.

When word spread that I was prepared to take in abandoned creatures on the land I bought in 1971, I had no idea that the small trickle of diseased, neglected or simply unwanted animals would become a flood that took over the land, creating a twelve-acre sanctuary housing more than six hundred animals today. When people started approaching me, asking to work for free as volunteers to help care for the strays and rescue animals that were starting to arrive, I had no idea that they would become the loyal and hardworking tribe that I now call my motley crew. I had no idea that the Barby Keel Animal Sanctuary charity would eventually be born, creating a legal entity that will continue to protect some of our region's most vulnerable creatures long after I am gone. I sold the land, the premises, the buildings and the infrastructure to the charity for £1 in order to secure the charity's future, to create a legacy that will continue day in, day out, giving a home to those who are unwanted and abandoned.

Material things have never interested me. When I was a young woman, I was offered a modelling contract in London. It was a big deal, lots of money and glamour, something that most young girls would dream of. I barely hesitated before refusing it. Looks and fortunes have never interested me; they hold no value and no seduction for me. I have never yearned to travel, never lusted after expensive clothes, designer labels or luxury cars. I have never regretted turning down that opportunity, though it could've created an entirely different life for me. The only thing that has ever mattered to me was animal welfare. Perhaps I've lived a very sheltered life, and perhaps for many people, it would be unbearably limited, living on a sanctuary I'd created, attached like an umbilical cord to the animals that we all cared for, being here each and every day, including Christmas, to take in unwanted, abused or neglected animals. Perhaps it would crush others, but it has been everything to me. My life, my heart and my soul are embedded within this land, these people, and most of all, within the care of the creatures we house, some of which live out their lives with us.

We can't rehome every animal that comes to us. Some have been so badly beaten, so abused and neglected that all we can do is help them live out their last days in dignity and with proper care. It is hard not to hate humans when animals come to us with cigarette burns on their fur, their limbs broken, their weak bodies trembling, traumatized from a life spent being shouted at or hit. It is very hard not to react when people bring animals to us they simply don't want any more, as if the little lives they have in their arms aren't worth the commitment.

When I feel despair at the actions of human beings, I force myself to look around at the twenty or so workers who come every day to clean out the rabbit hutches or the cattery, administer food and water to the kennels, take the dogs out for walks, or help build outbuildings or store cupboards to house everything we need to run the sanctuary.

I look at these people, who work for nothing except the reward of helping animals, who give their time and patience to help desperately sick creatures, and I know that there is love and kindness in the world. I first saw it when I sat at my father's side, helping him to care for mongrels, kittens and even a monkey once. I see it when I look at the faces of those who work here, the devotion that drives them to give their time and energy to help the animals who are brought here.

We know that not every injured or abandoned creature finds its way to us, and it is a hard truth to acknowledge that there are plenty that we can't help, that we can't love back to life, and that knowledge breaks my heart.

My sanctuary is a place where tragedy, comedy and a deep love for animals is present every single day. From day one, I vowed that I would never turn an animal away, and that policy remains today. However traumatized or sick an animal is, we take it in. No matter how it has been treated, what behavior it displays, what condition it is in, we open our arms and our hearts and do whatever we can to give it the love it may never have received.

The sanctuary is a special place. There are six hundred mouths to feed and water each day, and we are home to every kind of creature, from dogs to peacocks to pigs, all waiting to be loved back to health, or simply loved and cared for if they are beyond human help. It is a privilege to help as we do, to create a space where no animal is denied treatment or care.

It is not an entirely unselfish act. As I care for an animal, so I am cared for, in ways I am unable to explain. Over and over again I see animals restored to health by the simple act of being loved, and the people who do this are, in turn, healed or nurtured, rewarded in some way that lies beyond words.

I want to share the heartbreak and the joy of being an animal fosterer, to demonstrate the reason why no animal is ever turned away from the Barby Keel Animal Sanctuary because miracles can happen—we see them every day.

Chapter 1
LOCKED IN

"**B**ad dog! You little git, look what you've done!" The man's voice thundered over my head, stopping me in my tracks. Instantly alert, I looked over and saw my master had thrown the door open. A large, tall, red-faced man with a cap on his head and Wellington boots caked in mud on his feet, his face looked furious. He made two great strides into the room where I had been playing happily, absorbed in chasing a fly around the rooms of the large house I lived in. It was a spacious place with plenty of enticing smells, new things to discover and outside there was a large field I could run around in, which was heaven. I was only a young puppy and everything was still new and exciting. This wasn't, though. The man's voice was scaring me. Confused, I cocked my head to one side, but my master had a look of pure menace on his face. He bent over and picked up a cushion I'd been chewing, and looked over at the chair I'd knocked over during my play. The stuffing from the cushion was scattered all over the floor, an ornament had smashed on the wooden floor and I'd left a trail of muddy paw prints across the sofa I'd leapt on. I saw what I'd done and my heart swooped down into my tummy. I knew I would be in trouble as I'd been a messy boy, again.

I gave an exploratory wag of my tail, wanting desperately to appeal to him, to make him soften, to reach down and tickle me under the chin, but if anything, he looked scarier. He took another pace forward. I could smell the cigarette smoke on his clothes and I cowered as he approached.

"I've had enough, d'ya hear me?" He shouted again, and it hurt my ears. I realized I was in terrible trouble. I wagged my tail again, staring up at him, desperately hoping that he would stop. I couldn't help it. I was always trying to get some show of affection from him; after all, he was my owner. So far in my short life there'd been little kindness shown to me, and I was starved of attention and strokes. Even though I was unsure of the welcome I would get, I bounded up to my master, who was looming over me now, my big puppy paws making my movements clumsy.

It was a mistake. As I reached him, he glared down at me, and as his eyes met mine, I saw there was no kindness there, no affection or love, just utter fury. I wagged my tail again, desperate for a kind smile or a quick stroke to make everything better. Instead, my master smiled a twisted smile, which made me stop in my tracks. My tail stopped moving. My ears flattened back, and in that split second as I hesitated, the blow landed.

I yelped as I was forced back, the force of the swipe knocking me over. My face hurt from the impact, and my head was spinning. What had I done? Why was he so cruel to me? My heart was racing now. I was scared, terrified of this brute. I backed off, my ears back, my sense of dread growing by the second. I kept moving back until the wall stopped me. I was trapped and shaking violently. The man put his head down level with mine. I whined a little, partly from my throbbing face and partly from fear. His eyes were mean.

"You've ripped the sofa, AGAIN. You've trashed this house, AGAIN. That's it, you're goin' back outside. You can't live in 'ere anymore."

His voice was harsh, his manner furious. I didn't know what he was saying to me but I cowered in fear, desperately wanting to get away from him. My tail was firmly between my legs, my ears back in fright as he reached towards me. Would he hurt me again?

Instead, he grabbed me roughly. I yelped again, his fingers digging painfully into my fur as he marched towards the door, flinging it open with his other arm. I was wedged inside the crook of his arm, his arm gripping my middle tightly. I tried to squirm but stopped when he shouted again.

The shock of being suddenly greeted by the night air silenced me. It was the kind of spring evening when the air is still crisp, the winter chill still present. The air was thick with the smoke from a wood burner and I could smell a sharp scent from foxes and other nighttime creatures. My owner kept going, striding across the yard until we came to one of the outbuildings. It was only then that I realised what was happening. I started to struggle again but he held me tighter, hissing at me to be quiet. I was squirming with fear by the time we reached the rough wooden door, behind which lay my worst nightmare, a place where I'd been left many times before, a place of absolute darkness.

"Get in there, you won't be comin' out for a while, not until I've decided what to do with ya . . ."

The words meant nothing to me, but I got the sense of them. I knew, somehow, that my future was in jeopardy, and I was powerless to do anything about it.

I whimpered as he threw open the door, the stench of mold, rotten wood and my own urine and feces greeting me. As I tried to cower into his arms, my owner threw me roughly to the floor and strode out without another word, slamming the door shut behind him and leaving me standing alone, quivering with fright, in the pitch black of that terrible place.

I heard the man's footsteps retreat across the yard, and then there was silence, broken only by the screech of an owl close by that made me cry. I couldn't help but tremble in fear and loneliness, the cold biting at me. The only sounds were my whimpering, the scratching of mice, and the rustle of old musty leaves as I sat there on the damp earthen floor.

The stench of my surroundings stung my nose, reminding me of all the times I'd been dumped here before when I'd done something wrong. I never knew what it was that upset my master so much. I was a big puppy, prone to knocking things over, galloping awkwardly through the house and grounds with the master's other dogs, but I never deliberately damaged anything, I never got grumpy or cross, never tried to bite anyone or chase them. My predicament was a mystery to me, which made it all the harder to bear. My face was throbbing and I was thirsty. There was no water to drink, no bowl of food to eat either. Panic rose again in me. The darkness was unrelenting. I couldn't see my own paws in the blackness. I ran to the door, scratching at it, crying as I tried to open it, to find a crack of light, anything that might set me free. I sniffed at the floor, pawing at the cold, hard floor in the hope of finding a way to open it. When I finally realized I was hopelessly trapped, I started to howl in fear and misery. I couldn't see anything. The terrors of the night lay before me and I crumbled inside. I barked, I howled, I whimpered all night but no-one came.

The blackness filled my head. I used my sense of smell to navigate towards the moldy old sofa that had been dumped in the building. The air was cold and damp. I shivered as I crept onto the sofa, the only place I could curl up and wait for the morning to come, shutting my eyes against the enveloping darkness, all the time hoping that someone would let me out.

Hours later, I was curled up on the sofa when I finally heard the sound of footsteps approaching. The cocks had started crowing out in the yard so I knew that morning had come, though there was little light creeping into my prison. Suddenly the door burst open and my master stood in the doorway.

I jumped up and bounded over, filled with joy at the prospect of being released, my tail wagging, my tongue lolling out. I didn't care that he'd treated me so cruelly, I just wanted to be free, and I was ready to lavish him with devotion for letting me out again.

"Don't even think about it. There's yer food, you're staying in 'ere."

I didn't understand his words, but his voice still sounded angry. Nonetheless, I was happy to see him. He shoved a bowl of food and another of water down by the door, and I tried to nuzzle against him, my whole body overcome with relief that I wouldn't have to endure another second in this horrible place.

My joy turned to horror as his boot found my body.

"Get back. Bloody dog!" he growled, kicking me aside.

"You're not comin' out. I've had enough of ya boy, d'ya hear me? Enough. I'm gettin' rid of ya and when I've decided what to do, I'll be back."

I didn't understand, but I could feel the pain I was in. The hard toe of his boot had knocked the breath from my body, and before I knew it, the door had slammed and I was left bewildered and crying, still trapped, still frightened, and all alone.

What had I done to upset him? I was a happy, playful dog. I loved nothing more than chasing the other grown-up dogs around the fields, but surely that couldn't be wrong?

I slumped down, all the joy I had felt just minutes before draining away, filled with dread as I wondered how much longer I'd be there, or even whether I'd ever come out again. The shock of the disappointment, the slammed door and the prospect of staying in this horrible place in the dark that frightened me, was too much for me. I started shaking from nose to tail, my ears pricked up, listening for every sound, hoping against hope that my owner would come back for me.

It was a long, long wait before he did. I had no idea how much time had passed before the door finally opened again. I dragged my head up from my paws, blinking in pain at the small shaft of sunlight that had entered the room so abruptly. The man was standing there, a cigarette dangling from his lips. He didn't say anything this time but walked towards me, his face menacing. I watched him nervously, trembling, unsure whether to wag my tail or keep my head down in case he hit me again. The light made my eyes sore and I realized I must've been in that outbuilding for a long time. I'd had no toys to play with, little food to eat, only a bowl shoved in here and there with barely enough time to make a run for it at the open door. I had become resigned to the dark, the terribly blackness that kept me curled tightly in a ball, wishing my ordeal would end.

This time, the man scooped me up more gently than he had before, and carried me out. I licked his face, which was rough with stubble, and wagged my tail a little, wondering if he'd forgiven me and everything was alright now.

Instead of heading towards the house, he carried on walking and we reached his van. Opening the boot, he put me down inside a large cardboard box, which puzzled me. He left the flaps open at the top but I still didn't like the feeling of being trapped again. I started to whine to show my master I didn't like it.

"Stop moaning, it's for yer own good," the man barked at me.

It was clear that there would be no love, no tenderness at all from him. I had no choice. I didn't want to upset him again because I was scared of what he might do, so I settled down. At least there was a blanket and a chew toy in there, so I tried not to whimper as the van started to move off, the crunch of gravel under its tires signalling our departure. I was confused now rather than scared, wondering what on earth the man was doing, and, more importantly, where he was taking me.

As the van drove off, I stuck my head out of the box, catching a glimpse of the house and outbuildings where I'd undergone my punishment, the fields that seemed to go on forever and even some of the other dogs who were bounding around playfully. I sighed a little, hopeful that this time my master would be taking me somewhere better. My loyalty had not been crushed by my punishment, I was ready to forgive, so desperate for love was I. I did not know it, but that was the last time I'd ever set eyes on my home.

Chapter 2

DUMPED

The sound of blackbirds singing the dawn chorus in the ash trees that lined the far end of my site woke me up. As soon as my eyes were open, before I'd so much as stretched or indulged in a yawn, Bessie and Paddington, two of my four beloved dogs, were already sniffing around my face, gently nudging me to get up and feed them. Bessie was a white, black and brown corgi, while Paddington was a collie cross. Both dogs had been dumped at my shelter, and now they shared my home with me.

Hercules, a huge Saint Bernard, tried to join them by trying to climb up on my double bed that I shared with Bessie and Paddington, but the great bulk of him was too much and I playfully pushed him away, somehow managing to sit up. Hercules had been brought in after his owner found him too large to handle. A couple of people had shown an interest in him, coming to look at him, but his size was off-putting, and somehow they always went home with a smaller, more manageable dog. I used to say to Hercules that he was with me "by default."

Wobbly, a beautiful small Labrador crossed with either a whippet or greyhound, appeared, jumping up and starting to lick my face. Wobbly had been abandoned when he was just weeks old, left out by the gate one summer evening, and it had been pure chance that one of the sanctuary volunteers had been walking by only minutes after the owner had vanished and spotted the little creature. Wobbly was a tiny black ball when he arrived, so small that I would carry him around inside my bra, an action that gave him his name!

I suppose people might think me eccentric, but I've always been surrounded by animals, and to my way of thinking, carrying one on me was no different to a mother carrying her baby in a sling.

My earliest memories as a young girl, a stick-thin, grumpy-faced, brown-haired little urchin, center around the pets and strays that found themselves living with my mother, father, older brother Peter and, later, my younger sister Pam, who arrived when I was ten years old, a happy surprise for my parents.

Rex was the first love of my life. He was a scruffy, handsome (in my eyes) mongrel with a permanent lopsided grin on his face. He was brought home by my father one day after seeing him roaming the streets of Eastbourne in Sussex, where we lived. It was the year the Second World War ended and the bunting from VE Day was still hanging, albeit wonkily by now, from the windows of the shops and houses in our town. Pam had just been born, and although I was thrilled to have a baby sister, it was the animals that were truly in my heart at that young age of ten.

"He's beautiful. Can he be mine? Please, pleeeease?" I wailed at my mother as I flung my school satchel in a corner of the lounge and sprinted into the garden with the dog that had greeted me on my doorstep.

"Mind you don't get his dirty paws on my clean floors. Get that *thing* outside or I'll chase it out with my broom," Mum shouted as she thundered towards me, her hands on her aproned hips, a permanent scowl on her face. Pam was nowhere to be seen so I assumed she'd been put down for a nap, which meant Mum was on the prowl. I dashed past her, knowing that she hated the motley collection of animals that Dad brought home from goodness knows where every week.

"Dad has no right bringing that thing here," she called after me.

"Yes he does, so there!" I shouted back at her over my shoulder, knowing there'd be hell to pay later for my cheek. I think I even blew a raspberry at her. I really was a rat bag at that age, and I had little affection for the woman who had brought me into the world. I had no sympathy for her dislike of Dad's rescue creatures. She made it very clear that she bore their company with ill-disguised bad grace.

Dad, normally a mild-mannered man who was distinctly under her thumb, would never back down when it came to the animals he was saving. His passion and commitment for them meant he would risk her displeasure again and again, Mum clattering the pots in the kitchen loudly to make her feelings known, or emptying out his pipe with the pointed gesture of a put-upon saint to make the point that if she had to put up with his animals, then she would make sure he'd forgo the nightly pipe he enjoyed.

I'd watched the power struggles between my parents warily over the years, always wondering when Mum would turn on me and I'd get it in the neck. My brother Peter, two years older than me and as different as you can imagine with golden hair and a beatific smile, would always be the one to help distract me from my worries by helping me to feed our pets and carrying the sacks of hamster or rabbit food, so that most of the time I was able to stay inside my animal-loving bubble, my place of safety and sanctuary where the care of the animals came first. The two of us spent many happy hours petting and stroking the various animals we shared our home with, drip-feeding baby birds who'd dropped from the hedgerows, and making sure we were as far as possible away from the troubled marriage we lived alongside. Many years later, Dad left our mother and came to live with me, at first in my flat in Eastbourne, then in a separate trailer on my site, and he was just the same, lending a hand to look after the animals that found their way to us over the years.

"Come on, Barby, let's play with him together," I heard Peter call as he clattered into the house after me, his hobnail boots echoing on the wooden floors.

I turned, beaming at him. The sight of my brother was enough to make most of my troubles vanish in an instant. His tie was askew, his hair ruffled after his day at school, but to me, he looked wonderful.

"Okay Peter, I'll race you." I giggled before haring off, making Mother scream all the harder, but we'd heard it so many times, it was like water off a duck's back by now.

From the moment we met, Rex seemed to gravitate straight to me. He'd jumped up at me when I crashed open the front door, which made me shriek with surprise and delight. I chased him out into the scrubby bit of garden at the back of the tiny terraced house, which comprised an area of grass about two meters square, a shed at the end that had been requisitioned by Dad as his store space for keeping animal feed, pieces of wood he could build hutches or runs from, and a big coil of chicken wire.

Rex barked, jumping and rolling on the ground, as Peter and I threw a ball for him, laughing with glee at our newfound friend.

"He's mine, though," I said to Peter sternly as he rubbed the dog's belly. Peter shrugged. There were plenty of other animals for him to help me with so he wasn't too bothered. He loved them but he was never mad about them like me and Dad.

"I'm calling him Rex because he's a king of dogs," I added stoutly. That was probably the only time my Latin lessons ever came in useful.

"Rex, come here boy," I called, and sure enough, to my delight, he came over, his funny face looking like he was smiling at me, his honey-colored fur sticking up all over the place.

"You really are the scruffiest, funniest-looking dog," I said softly, stroking his rough ears and tickling him under the chin.

Rex cocked his head to one side.

"He looks like he's listening!" I laughed.

Mother called Peter and me in for tea, and so, reluctantly, we left Rex chewing the ball outside while we trooped in, knowing we'd get a telling-off dished out to us along with the meat pie and beans from Dad's allotment.

At the time, Rex wasn't the only creature sheltering in our wholly inadequate space. There was a menagerie of creatures, such as a hamster who lived in the lounge in a makeshift cage, several cats prowling the area, who came into the kitchen to sleep overnight by the warm oven, a wounded seagull in a box on the kitchen worktop and an injured bird that needed our attention living in the shed. Each morning and evening, I would spoon-feed the bird, carefully dripping milk into its quivering beak. Dad thought its wing was broken so he'd bound it up with bandages and each day we peered at the tiny creature, willing it to get better.

Suddenly I felt a large shaggy paw on my knee and I realized I'd been caught up in my memories.

"Rex is long gone, darling," I mused to Paddington, whose doleful eyes looked up at me.

I looked down at the dogs and burst out laughing. All four of them were sitting expectantly in front of me, waiting to be fed and let outside.

"Come on then, let's get up and get going before the day's half gone," I said, scattering the dogs as I walked through to the kitchen.

Home for me and my dogs was a large but leaky trailer on the land I owned, which I'd named Pipzedene as a tribute to the four animals I'd owned when we'd first moved in: Pip the spaniel, Zede the Alsatian and Dene the Bush Baby. None of the animals were with me anymore, and it was my way of keeping their memories alive.

Outside the cockerels started to crow.

"You're too late, I'm already up," I muttered as I put down four bowls for the dogs and watched in amusement as they descended like a pack of wolves onto the food.

I grabbed a handful of bread and headed across the paddock, which housed our three resident horses, to the patch of land where I routinely fed two seagulls each morning.

At 6 am promptly, the two gulls, who I'd nicknamed Elvis and Pebbles, would settle on the electricity pylon that ran overhead and wait for their feed.

"Here you go, one slice for you, Elvis, and another for you, Pebbles . . ." I said, scrunching up the bread into crumbs and watching it fall to the floor in a shower.

In an instant, the birds swooped down, pecked at the offering, then just as suddenly, rose back up into the sky. I watched as they disappeared over the landscape, heading towards the coast just a couple of miles due south. From my current position, all I could see was countryside, its green acres dotted with hedgerows and trees, radiant in the morning light.

It was still a bit nippy out this early, so I hurried back to my makeshift home to make a cup of tea and wait for my trusted friend Diane to arrive and start the work of the day.

Diane had begun as a temporary volunteer years earlier, after seeing an article in a local free paper saying I needed help feeding our forty cats. She had been to Sainsbury's with her parents and bought a load of cat food to donate, and rang the bell to hand it over. I came to the gate, took one look at Diane, and took an instant liking to her. She was as rough and ready as me, and she'd been helping out ever since.

Diane was a well-built, strong woman with wisps of blond hair poking out of the woolly hat she wore whatever the weather, and I knew she'd be here, dependable and hard-working, by 6:30 am at the very latest.

I sat down, a cup of tea in my hand, listening to the sounds of the ducks, geese, chickens, horses, dogs, cats and various assorted other creatures, waking up and starting a new day. Dad poked his head around the door to say "Good morning," and I offered him the cuppa I'd already made for him. We sat together in companionable silence as the skies filled with sound.

That day began no differently from any other. Diane appeared and together we fed the horses, goats and pigs, before turning our attention to the cats that needed medication. Each morning me and Di would head to the makeshift hospital, checking the room where the poorly cats were kept. The smell always hit us first as the litter trays would be full and cleaning them would take a good hour. When that was done, we'd go through the list from the vet, checking which cats needed doses of whatever meds they were prescribed. We had diabetic cats, several recovering from surgery and one that had an abscess in her mouth that we were administering antibiotics to. The whole process took much of the morning, but I couldn't stay with Diane for long as I'd promised one of our volunteers

I'd check the rabbits, which desperately needed a new hutch as we were rapidly running out of space. By 11 am, both Diane and I needed a break, and I radioed her over our walkie talkie system, as she was still with the cats and I was ensconced with the rabbits, to meet for a cup of tea at my trailer in ten minutes.

"Right you are, Barby," she replied.

I thought I'd nip over to feed the pigs on the way back. I was just carrying a load of out-of-date buns and bagels over to the pigsty when I heard the sound of running feet.

"Quick, Barby, someone's at the gate," Diane panted as she came to a halt.

I was puzzled. "We're not expecting anyone, dear. Will you go and see what it is?"

Diane turned on her heels and ran up to the gate that I'd recently installed.

Someone arriving unexpectedly always gave us a real sense of urgency. Time and time again, people would arrive to dump animals at our doorstep. At best, they would ring the bell and hand them over, but it was not unheard of for people to simply tie the animal to the gatepost or even leave them on the side of the track as a way of abandoning their animals anonymously.

Thankfully, the animals were usually healthy and it was nothing to panic about, but between us, we'd found enough terribly injured, neglected or sick creatures to justify Diane's urgency.

I stood, shading my eyes from the afternoon sunshine, squinting in the direction Diane had run off in. Just as she reached the gate, I heard the loud squeal of tires speeding on the gravel, followed by the sound of a motor engine revving and a vehicle leaving rather too quickly.

"Oh blimey, I'm coming too," I called, rushing over.

This didn't look good. Diane had the gate open, and she was attempting to pick up something that looked like a large cardboard box.

My heart was pounding, both from running and from fear at what we might be about to find.

"What the hell is that?" I asked anxiously.

"Help me get it inside," Diane replied, abruptly. From the sound of scrabbling claws, it was clear that there was a frightened animal inside.

"Oh Christ, we'll have to drag it inside. We can't open it outside the gate as whatever it is might run off in fright . . ."

"Or attack us," Diane interjected.

We both grabbed a corner of the box, and half dragged, half carried it through the gate and onto the sanctuary land. It wasn't so much heavy as awkward to move.

"It's in," I said with relief, "now bolt that gate and let's see what we've got here."

Somehow, the idea of an animal possibly leaping out or biting me as I opened the box didn't frighten me one bit. I was to desperate to know what we were dealing with, and my mind immediately assumed the worst, given that the owner had just dumped the box here. I felt sick at the thought of discovering some abused or disease-ridden creature inside, and I knew that once this was over, I'd feel utter rage at the manner of this creature's abandonment.

There was some tape across the top of the box, which I pulled off, and opening the flaps with some delicacy, I peered inside.

Staring back at me from the depths of this large, dark container, was the saddest sight. A tiny trembling, black rough-haired, straggly-looking puppy looked up at me, his ears flat against his head, whimpering softly as he gazed back at me, his big brown eyes wide with fear.

My eyes filled with tears at the sight of this vulnerable, terrified creature, and I tried to soothe him as best I could.

"Welcome, little one," I said quietly, "it's ok, you're safe now. No one's going to hurt you here. We're here to look after you, I promise."

Chapter 3

No Home to Call His Own

I reached into the box to gently stroke the little creature, but the pup shied away from me, just as I would expect from any abused dog, especially one so young.

"Come here, beautiful, and let me give you a cuddle," I whispered softly, making sure to keep my voice as low as possible. I didn't want to risk overwhelming this puppy, and I deliberately made my movements slow, my voice calm and low so as not to startle him.

"Oh, he's a lovely boy," said Diane, looking over my shoulder.

"He's a scared little thing, that's for sure," I sighed, trying to coax him out from his dark prison.

"Who put you in this horrid box, eh, boy?" I murmured. "Who would do such a thing? You'd much rather be running about my fields smelling all the plants and animals, wouldn't you?"

Finally, I managed to get hold of the trembling dog and felt him flinch as I pulled him out.

"I think he might have an injury or wound somewhere as

he reacted when I touched him," I said to Diane, "but he's a gentle pup, and it bodes well that he's letting me carry him. Let's take him to the trailer and check him over, Di."

I started walking back towards the trailer, then stopped short, remembering my mutts.

"Would you clear out the other dogs before we get there so we don't frighten him any more than he is already?"

"Of course, Barby, give me a moment." Diane rushed off ahead of me.

"There, there, poor boy. You really are the scraggiest thing I've ever seen . . ." I cooed at the little bundle in my arms. I couldn't help but chuckle at the sight of him. He had black wiry fur, eyes that twinkled back at me despite his obvious fear, and I could see he was going to be a very big dog from his enormous paws, which seemed comically large in proportion to his skinny body. His coat was rough and coarse, and the hair around his eyes was long and wiry.

"Well, boy, I'm guessing you have some Irish Wolfhound in you," I said to him, making his face turn up to me. I smiled, already sensing a sweetness to his temperament from the way he was letting me, a total stranger, carry him, even though it was obvious that he was hurt or injured in some way. Irish Wolfhounds are renowned for their lovely personalities.

"All clear," Diane said at the door of my trailer. As she said it, Bessie and Hercules appeared at my side, sniffing at the creature in my arms.

"Get away," I said gruffly, "This one's not for you to play with."

Carefully, I took the puppy inside, making sure to shut the

door after me so that my dogs couldn't get in, and this little one couldn't get out. I laid him down on a rug Di had placed on my kitchen table, and we both took a moment to inspect him.

His fur was matted and straggly but he looked healthy enough. I picked up one of his large paws to check it was free of cuts or stones and he pulled it back, letting out a little whine.

"Not many pups like their feet being touched," I told him gently, "but we have to have a look to make sure you're alright."

"He's a handsome boy, isn't he? What do you reckon, Irish Wolfhound?" Diane speculated. There wasn't anything Diane didn't know about animals, or the trees and plant species around the site. She was a mine of information, absorbing facts out of thin air, and sharing her infinite wisdom with me and the rest of the volunteers.

"I was right, boy!" I beamed, scratching gently under the dog's chin. "Yes, I think he's got wolfhound in him. He's already got the long legs and it's clear he'll grow into a large dog. I need to finish checking him over, make sure there's nothing major we need to call the vet out for," I said. At that moment, the door of the trailer swung open and Ian appeared.

"Shut that blinking door, will you!" I shouted in alarm. "Otherwise the dogs will get in."

"What's going on, Barby?" Ian asked, leaning against the door. Ian was a young man with an absolute passion for saving animals. He'd been so driven to save them that he'd been an active member of the hunt saboteur movement in the 1980s,

disrupting hunts long before the sport was banned, though
that was before his time at my sanctuary. Many of the young
men and women who ended up volunteering for me had some
experience of "hunt sabbing" in their past. Ian didn't stand
out because of that. It was his natural care for animals that
had appealed to me. Thanks to his activist past, he was in
touch with a vast community of committed animal welfare
people who organized animal rescues in places as diverse as
Africa and Russia, as well as the UK. His sabbing days were
behind him now but his allegiances had never changed and
he was a vegan long before it became more popular.

He wore a dirty cap that had seen better days, a large pair
of working boots with trousers tucked into them and a
T-shirt. He grinned at me as he stood there.

"Never you mind," I joked. I could always banter with Ian
as he never seemed to take anything seriously, except animal
welfare of course.

"Seriously, though, Barby, why didn't you bring him over
to the kennels? I could have had a look at him there?"

The pigsties where the dogs lived were a stone's throw from
my trailer, and Ian had been back from walking some of the
dogs when the puppy had been dumped, so it would've been
normal practice to involve him.

Ian walked over and ruffled the puppy's fur gently. It always
amazed me how loving and patient he was with the dogs, cats
and horses in his care. I also knew he was making fun of the
area we kept the dogs in because we didn't really have a proper
kennels yet; all we had were a few pigsties that I'd cleaned out
to make room for all the dogs that were brought in.

"You're a beautiful boy, aren't you, eh?" he said, smiling down at the puppy.

"Well, I'm off," Diane announced. "I've got to give the diabetic cats their medicine and check on the other hospital inmates. Look after this little fella, and I'll see you later."

As soon as Diane opened the door to leave, I could see Bessie trying to get her nose round the door.

"Shoo, Bessie, stay outside." I waved her off.

"Oh, and Barby? Whatever you do, don't fall in love with him. You've got four dogs already, and that's quite enough to be getting on with in a trailer . . ." Diane popped her head back round the door and grinned at me before disappearing again.

I laughed as I waved her off, but there was a grain of truth in her words.

"Don't you dare go and do what Di says and fall in love with this puppy, Barby," I thought to myself sternly as I watched Ian check him over. He was so careful, looking at his fur, checking for mange and hair loss, looking for bites or scratches. Then Ian touched his left flank and the pup visibly twitched.

"There you go, boy, there's nothing to worry about. We'll soon get you right," he said soothingly as he finished his inspection.

"He's got a bruise but I don't think it's serious; he'd be in way more pain if there was anything really wrong."

"Why has he got a bruise, though?" I frowned, stroking that rough fur. The puppy was sitting up now, his body still trembling but much more settled than when he first arrived.

"He may have been hit or kicked. It does look a bit like that. Luckily, there's nothing fundamentally wrong, but I'd get Stephen in if I were you, just to be sure. Sometimes bruises can suggest abuse and it's always better to be on the safe side."

Stephen White was based at the Claremont Veterinary Group in Sidley, a mile or so down the road. He was a serious man utterly devoted to animals, and he was highly rated for his care and knowledge among my motley crew.

"I'll call him this morning, though I doubt he'll come out here today at such short notice," I answered.

Ian nodded. "I've checked his mouth and that's clear. I've checked him over for sores, rashes or any other signs of infection, and I can't see anything. We'll need to clean out his ears and make sure he's properly groomed but he looks okay. I can't see any sign of disease or any other mistreatment, apart from the possible bruising."

We both looked at the dog sitting on my table. He stared back at us, his dark eyes like great pools of sadness.

"Who would abandon you, eh, boy," I couldn't help but say. He might not be the most elegant of dogs, but there was definitely something about him, a gentleness perhaps, which I warmed to immediately.

"Right, well, if you're happy to look after him for now, I've got the goats to feed," Ian announced, giving the puppy one final pat. "Did I tell you that we had a phone call from someone wanting to drop off a load of abandoned kid goats?"

"Why would someone have a load of baby goats to drop off without their mothers?" I asked in astonishment, temporarily distracted from the puppy.

"I've no idea, Barby, why does anyone dump any of their animals? Who knows? They're just lucky we're here to take them in." And with that, Ian disappeared out the door.

There was so much work to do each day at the sanctuary. What had started as taking in a few strays and homeless animals had become a full-time job, both in caring for them and in raising the funds to enable us to keep caring for them. We were incredibly lucky. The local community had got behind the shelter as it grew over the years, and continued to support us, though it was hard work juggling all the balls needed to keep us afloat. Despite that, the shelter was exactly as I thought a sanctuary ought to be, with animals roaming free across the land. It was normal for donkeys to wander in front of the trailer, or a horse to poke its nose through my window.

I sighed. "Well, I'd better ring the vet. No, don't worry, I'm not going to leave you . . ." I said quickly as the dog started to make whimpering noises when I moved away.

His big eyes peered at me as I picked up the phone and dialed.

When the vet answered, I explained the situation, smiling at the sight of this adorable mutt who was looking confused but behaving so well. To my relief, the vet had an opening and was free to come over in an hour's time.

"Did you hear that, boy, the vet is coming to check you over and make sure you're healthy before we find someone who can take you in. In the meantime, we've got lots of time for cuddles."

As I sat next to the pup at the table, his tail gave a small wag, and he turned and licked my outstretched hand. I stroked his ears, with their tufts of black stringy hair, and rubbed under his chin. Letting me stroke him was another good sign that he wasn't psychologically or emotionally damaged by whatever treatment he'd experienced.

Rescuing an animal is an uncertain business. If an animal is dumped or abandoned, very often we have no idea how they have been treated, or whether they've been beaten or abused. Even if there are no obvious signals such as malnourishment, cuts and scars, or aggression, we still can't rule out the possibility that the animal has suffered.

I've always found it incredibly sad that we don't know a dog's history when they come to us in the way this one had. Without any information, it sometimes felt like we were blind in the face of the issues an unwanted pet could present.

Luckily, it seemed that this puppy had survived his ordeal rather better than expected. As well as letting me stroke and pat him, he was curious, looking around the room, taking in everything he could see, and though he was clearly still full of trepidation, he had started to show affection, and more importantly, he was able to receive it.

"I think you'll be alright, little one, but you've got no home to call your own, have you boy?" With that, the pup reached up to lick my face, his little tail now wagging furiously.

"Stop kissing me," I grinned, picking him up and cuddling him. "We'll find you a home, don't you worry . . ."

Chapter 4
CHECKING PUPPY OVER

"Barby, Stephen's here. I'll bring him over to you." Diane's voice crackled over the walkie talkie.

"Thank you, dear," I replied.

As I moved, the pup snuggled further into my arms. Dad chuckled when he saw the dog's reaction.

"He knows where he's happy."

I smiled over at the dear man. He had aged recently but still had that gentle loveliness oozing from him. He was a true gentleman, a man devoted to animals, and someone I had always relied upon. I liked him living near me so I could keep an eye on him, and he was a good worker.

"Right, I'm off out," he announced, standing up and giving the puppy an affectionate pat. "I'm helping Di in the cattery today, then I might have a look at the fencing on the far field. I noticed some of it was starting to lean over."

"Thanks, Dad," I replied, as the dog snuggled even further into my clothing. I turned to look down at him, and laughed. "You're quite a weight, boy. Lots of dogs don't get to be your size until they're fully grown, but something tells me you've still got a lot more growing to do."

A few seconds after Dad left, I heard the vet's voice as he greeted my father. Then Stephen poked his head round the trailer door.

"Knock, knock . . ." the young vet said.

"I'm in the kitchen," I called. "Come in and look at what turned up at our gate this morning."

Stephen was wearing his customary white coat and carrying a large bag. After seeing the dog, I'd asked him to check out the cats in our Feline Immunodeficiency Virus (FIV) section. This area was caged off on all sides, including chicken wire across the top, to stop any of the cats escaping. They had the cat equivalent of the AIDS virus, and we had only recently started to take them in. The cats were kept inside to stop them infecting other felines through fighting or mating. It also protected the sick cats from being infected by viruses that a normal healthy animal would fight off. Their immune systems had been compromised and so they were kept separate, in a large run with trees and branches to keep them entertained, with lots of rugs and blankets to keep them cosy and warm too.

The cats suffering with FIV were usually brought over to the UK by a charity that finds them in Romania, and we were one of the few places, if not the only place, that took them in. They needed a lot of care, though, and our monthly vet bills were starting to run into the thousands of pounds.

"Well, what do we have here? You're a handsome boy, aren't you?" Stephen put down his vet's bag and came straight to us. I handed the pup to him. The puppy was good as gold, he didn't wince this time and although he submitted to the vet's checks with a small wag of his tail and a lick on Stephen's arm, I could see the little dog was still trembling.

"He was dumped here by goodness knows who in a bloody cardboard box!" I didn't usually swear, but remembering the events of the morning I suddenly felt my anger rise as I watched the puppy shaking. He was so young, so vulnerable, and yet someone had clearly treated him badly.

"Whoever it was stuck him in a box, drove him to the gate, then left before we could see who it was or ask any questions. Why do people behave like that? It makes me mad!"

I was really fuming now.

Stephen carried on checking the pup. "Well, Barby, we'll probably never know why someone ditched him but I can say that he's in very good condition, considering." He stroked the pup's head and was rewarded by another lick on his hand.

"I know, Stephen, it just seems so wrong. Why take on a dog if you're going to abandon it at the drop of a hat?"

Even though fostering animals meant I had to keep a cool head and be very careful about not judging people, sometimes the injustice of it all broke through.

At the sanctuary, we knew how distressing it was to give up a beloved pet through illness, poverty or age. We knew that we were, for many people, a last resort, and that it was a heart-rending decision to leave their animal with us. In cases like this, though, it was clear that this definitely wasn't the case.

"No animal lover would leave a puppy in a box by a gate.

What if we hadn't seen it for a day or two? The puppy could've been made really ill through dehydration or lack of food. There was nothing inside the box that suggested the owner really cared. There was a blanket, but certainly no food or water." I sighed, finally running out of steam.

It was an emotional rollercoaster being an animal fosterer, but for some reason, this little puppy made me feel even more protective than usual.

Stephen was staring at me, waiting for me to finish.

"Sorry, I think this little one has got under my skin. He's so gentle and sweet. Look at his eyes, they're gorgeous, like liquid chocolate . . ."

I heard myself speak and knew that I was falling head over heels for this puppy. I had to rein my feelings in. I had no room for another dog. It was best to get him checked over, be given a clean bill of health, and then I could ring around all the people who'd come to me asking for a puppy to take on.

"Well, I'd estimate he's about ten months old, and he's definitely got some Briard in him. Irish Wolfhound crossed with Briard, I think. It means he'll be a big dog."

"Is that what you are, little one, a big hunting dog, eh?" I crooned, and the puppy wagged his tail and submitted to me stroking his rough ears.

I knew a fair bit about both those breeds, having come across them over the years. Irish Wolfhounds were bred thousands of years ago to assist soldiers in wartime, and were large and fast enough to drag men off chariots and horses. They had also been used as hunting dogs, with wolves, deer and wild boar as their prey, and they were the tallest breed of any dog.

Despite their fierce heritage, the hounds themselves made lovely family dogs, with sweet, adaptable natures, fierce loyalty and the ability to be trainable. Briards were similar in that they were bred in France as herding and guard dogs. They were shaggier than the wolfhounds, which explained this pup's longer, coarser hair. Intelligent and brave, Briards were used as working dogs in the First World War as sentries, messengers and even as medic dogs. They were often described as "hearts wrapped in fur" by dog breeders due to their affectionate nature and utter devotion to their owner. No wonder this puppy was such a sweet boy, he had love bred into his bones. I felt my heart sink at the thought of how difficult it would be to say goodbye to him.

"I can't see anything to worry you, Barby. He's a strong puppy, there are no signs of disease at all. He has a slight bruise on his left side but that already seems to be healing." Stephen gave the pup a last stroke, and picked up his bag.

"He seems healthy, though he is a bit scruffy and unloved-looking. You know where I am if you need any help with him. Right, time for me to check on the FIV cats and then the rabbits need their claws trimming. I'll pop in and see you before I go."

"Thank you for coming out," I called after him, already turning back to the dog in my care.

"Let's put you down on the floor while I start ringing round to find you a new home." I picked the creature up, feeling his warm doggy body against me as I carefully placed him on the floor of my temporary home.

He shivered as his large puppy paws found the surface, and as soon as I moved, he followed after me in his clumsy, awkward way. My heart melted as he stopped to sniff at one of the dog's bowls, leaping over it when he realized I'd moved away and into my large lounge space.

"You look like you're my shadow, pup," I mused as I started riffling through the pile of papers on my cabinet, which only seemed to get larger by the day.

"It's somewhere in here," I muttered to myself, as I scrabbled through the vet bills, letters from well-wishers, animal-fostering documents and agreements, fundraising requests, until, at last: "Ah ha, here it is."

I pulled out my large black diary and address book from under a pile of press cuttings. The local paper, the *Bexhill Observer*, had started to take a keen interest in my private sanctuary, and through publicity, was helping me to reach my ever-burdensome monthly budgets for running this place.

As I opened the diary, a shower of papers fell out.

"Damn and blast," I snorted, and instantly the puppy sprang back, a look of sheer terror on his gorgeous face. In that moment, I caught a glimpse of this little dog's past life, the experiences he must've had to end up so frightened of humans, to scare so easily after a mild curse by me.

"They frightened you, didn't they, boy?" I said, keeping my voice gentle and low as I held out my hand to the pup. He had backed off, and had been looking at me anxiously, but as the moment passed, he sniffed a little, started to walk over, though his ears were drooped and his face had lost that seemingly constant smiling expression.

"Poor boy, yes, that's it, come closer. I'm sorry I scared you, that must've been horrid," I said, whispering to him until he stopped trembling and looked up at me, his eyes filled with love this time. "Don't worry, boy, it's only a few bits of paper I haven't got round to filing. Come here, that's it." I pulled the dog to me and gave him a cuddle that I hoped reassured him.

Once he'd stopped shaking again, I picked up a ball that had rolled under the armchair and threw it to him. He seemed to look puzzled for a moment, then patted it with his funny, too-big-for-him paw.

"You've never played with a ball before, have you, eh," I said, more as a statement than a question. It was fascinating when the pieces of a jigsaw fell together and revealed small bits of an animal's past.

The pup sniffed it, rolled it a bit with one paw, then grabbed it in his mouth and came back to me.

"You learn quickly," I cried with delight, patting him as he wagged his tail delightedly.

For the next ten minutes, both of us were taken up with playing fetch, and it was a joy to see the puppy starting to play like a normal dog of his age. He had no problem with enjoying a game, and it was obvious that no one had ever taken the time to throw him a ball before. It was a sad realization, but at least I would find someone to care for him who would play with him, spend time each day taking him for walks, throwing sticks and generally showing him that the life of a young pup should be one of pleasure and fun.

Finally, after much fun and joyful barking, it was time to go back to the task in hand.

"Hello, dear, it's Barby. How are you?" I said to my friend Hettie, someone who supported the sanctuary regularly by donating money or buying fencing or feed for us, and who had been looking for a puppy as a companion dog.

"I've got an Irish Wolfhound cross, ten months old, and a real sweetie. Does he sound like the one for you?"

I listened to my friend's response. She ummed and ahhed before deciding he'd grow too big for her small home, but she wished me luck in finding somewhere for him.

"To be honest, I'd like him to go to a new home today as otherwise I might want to keep him," I confessed, making my friend laugh.

"You always want to keep all of them, Barby. Goodbye, dear."

I picked up the phone again and called a few people, with no luck. Then I spotted the names of a young couple who had called in to the site a few weeks earlier looking specifically for a puppy to adopt.

"Hello, this is Barby Keel from the animal sanctuary. Well, we've got a puppy who needs a home."

Just as I spoke I heard a crash. I turned round to see the pup looking over at me beseechingly. He'd knocked over a pile of books while leaping up at an insistent fly that had been buzzing annoyingly.

"Er, well, as I was saying, we have a gorgeous Irish wolf-hound puppy. Can you take him?"

"We'd love to come and see him. Can we come today?" The woman's voice sounded extremely eager.

"Yes, I think that'd be best. He's a big dog, part Briard, part wolfhound, so I warn you he won't be a tiny thing; he'll grow into a lovely big dog." I thought I'd better warn them first.

"We want a big dog, so that suits us perfectly," the woman replied. "We'll be there in half an hour."

I thanked them and rang off. "They're eager, and who can blame them?"

I looked over at him. He was already massive for a pup, and with his straggly black hair, that gawky gait with huge paws making him clumsy and eyes that smiled back at me, I found him irresistible.

"You're a beautiful boy," I laughed. He looked so comical as he stared back at me quizzically, cocking his head to one side.

"No, I cannot fall in love with you. Anyway, your new home awaits you," I added, as if this adorable pup could possibly understand, and far more firmly than I felt inside.

I could hear my other dogs sniffing around outside. It was getting close to their feeding time, but there was no way I would let them in, in case they frightened or overwhelmed this boy. I stared around the trailer, smiling as I recalled how this was only ever meant to be a temporary home for a few months until my partner Les and I rebuilt our house.

Les had been a charmer, a devilishly attractive man who swept me off my feet as a young woman. He wasn't tall but had golden hair, a square jaw and muscly frame. All the girls fancied him but it was me he chose, and together we'd come to look at this eight-acre site when I was thinking of buying land with the money I'd saved over the years, squirrelling away every spare penny I had whilst working as a waitress in an Eastbourne hotel.

It wouldn't have mattered what he'd thought of it. When I stepped out of my car, breathed in the smell of the spring grass, the gentle breeze singing through the trees, and saw the backdrop of the undulating countryside, I had already decided to buy it. That was in 1971, nineteen years before the Briard pup had arrived at my door, and together we'd built every fence that lined the land, every gate, every house and shed. It had been a labour of love, and many times I'd have to sell a possession to afford the cost of wooden stakes or animal feed.

Together, we'd built our own longhouse, a prefabricated home with a log burner at the center and the rooms fanning down each side. It was huge, and we'd put our heart and soul into painting the insides, tiling the kitchen and bathroom, all of which we fitted ourselves.

We hadn't lived there long when a visit from the Rother District Council planners killed our dreams of living there forever. Les hadn't applied for planning permission, and I hadn't thought to ask, so we were forced to take it down. The day the bulldozers came, I bundled Zede, Pip and various other dogs into my car and drove away, hearing the THUD, THUD of our home being shattered as I went.

That sound has never left me. My relationship with Les finished (though we remained friends), and from the day the bulldozers came, I had lived in a trailer on the site. I put down pots and pans each night through the autumn and winter to collect the rainwater that seeped through the holes in the metal roof. It wasn't much, but it was my home.

The puppy had become more confident and was sniffing his way around each room in the place. I had a large bedroom with a double bed, a kitchen space, and a lounge with enough room for a sofa and armchair, not forgetting the television. It wasn't Buckingham Palace, but it wasn't hardship either. I'd weathered many a winter storm in here, shivering next to the electric fire and praying that the trailer would last another year. I knew many people found my sacrifices strange, but for me, it had always been more important that my animals were safe and secure than worrying about where I was living. I didn't yet have the funds to rebuild, and until I did, I put up with it in the knowledge that every animal on my land had shelter, food and safety. I had always been barmy when it came to animals, and nothing was ever going to change that.

Just then, I heard another crash. I rushed into my bedroom to find my bedside lamp on the floor, and the puppy cowering in a corner. I couldn't help but chuckle.

"Who's a clumsy boy! Never mind, there's nothing to be scared of. Now, very soon, we're going to wrap you in a blanket and carry you to a car, and your new owners will take you home."

The pup came over to me, reassured that there would be no vengeance for the mess he'd caused. I let him lick my outstretched hand, grinning as he did.

"We're going to find a lovely home for you," I promised, hoping for his sake that he'd find an owner who would love him as much as I'd come to in a few short hours.

Chapter 5

SAYING GOODBYE

"He needs a name," Diane said, sitting down on a chair at my kitchen table. She looked filthy. Her hair was matted from the sweat of her day's efforts cleaning out the rabbit hutches with a volunteer called Carol. Carol was rather an eccentric woman with large spectacles and bobbed hair who lived in a home with her sixteen cats and sixteen tortoises. She'd converted the upstairs of her home to accommodate her menagerie. She would come in almost daily to look after the rabbits, and walk one of the dogs, a Staffie cross called Murphy, and was an absolute boon to my shelter. She helped Diane with many of the jobs such as cutting the rabbits' claws, and today, carrying new fencing over to the new farm animal enclosures to make pens for the five kid goats, which were due to arrive the next day.

I preferred to have my animals run free, but as more animals arrived, my volunteers, Diane included, had convinced me that I needed to create fenced areas for the different creatures, and after much persuasion I'd reluctantly agreed.

Diane had mud on her boots and her trousers looked like they'd seen better days. Despite her appearance, she was beaming as she stared lovingly at our latest arrival.

"It's the least you can do for that pup. You can't keep calling him puppy, and when you sign him out, you'll need to give him a name."

Together we were waiting for the young couple to arrive to take the dog with them. Whenever I rehomed a domestic animal such as a dog or cat, I made the new owners sign an agreement, showing official proof of the adoption, and listing their names, address and telephone details in case we ever needed to get in touch.

The forms were less complicated than the ones I'd devised for people giving up their animals, though no less important. When someone left their animal with us, we needed to know every aspect of their life so far, and those forms were exhaustive. There was a long list of questions for an owner to answer, asking about every part of the animal's care while in their homes, such as feeding patterns, behavioral issues, exercise regime, any veterinary visits or illnesses, whether the dog played well with children, with toys, whether it had been groomed regularly. It was an exhaustive list, ending with a disclaimer stating that the owner was giving up their legal rights to the animal.

I'd been stung before. One time, a man, whom I later heard via one of the volunteers was a heroin addict, gave up his dog for us to rehome as he knew he couldn't care for it properly. A month later, when the dog had been successfully settled in a loving new home, the man returned, demanding his dog back.

"He's mine and I want him back," he demanded aggressively, an ugly look on his face. He looked disheveled, with straggly black hair, boots that were falling apart, and a ripped T-shirt.

I didn't appreciate being spoken to that way on my own land, and far from being frightened of him, I was actually rather cross. This person had promised to donate some money to the sanctuary for taking in his dog as it hadn't been spayed, so we had to pay for that on top of caring for the animal, yet we'd never received anything.

At the time, there had been no official documents, as it just hadn't occurred to me that this situation could arise. Everything I'd done had been for the love of animals. I understood there were many reasons why people had to give them up and so I didn't want to distress them further by making them sign forms. How wrong I'd been.

"You'll go and get my dog, today, and bring him back here." The man looked threatening, but despite being only five foot tall with a tiny frame, I stood my ground. I could also be fierce when my back was against the wall.

"Now, look here. You can't come back here weeks after you hand over your dog to us and expect it still to be here. I told you it would be placed in a permanent home where it would be loved and cared for." I emphasized the word permanent to drive home my point.

"I don't give a crap what I said then—I want him back." The man had started to shout. I could smell stale booze com-

ing off him and his personal hygiene wasn't the best. I took
a step back. What would he do? Would he become violent?
He certainly looked as though he was building up to something, and I felt uneasy, but his behavior reaffirmed my belief
that we had absolutely done the best thing for his dog by rehoming it with a loving family.

I shook my head firmly, and he lunged towards me, but at
that moment, Arthur, one of the volunteers who walked the
dogs regularly, appeared out of nowhere.

"Everything okay, Barby?" he asked, his West Country
burr hidden beneath his stern tone of voice. Arthur was an
imposing man, at six foot tall with fair hair and a build well
used to shoveling hay, carrying large sacks of animal feed and
transporting fence posts across the land. In short, he had a
strong presence.

The heroin addict looked at both of us, realized he was
outnumbered and backed off.

"This isn't the last you'll see of me," he said as he left,
which made me shudder.

Once we'd made sure he was safely off the premises, I
turned to Arthur, the threat of the man's words dawning
on me.

"Arthur, what if he comes back at night? What will I do?"
Though I hated to admit it, the man had got to me.

"He won't. He's just a coward, and anyway you've got the
dogs to defend you, and your dad's on site. Nothing's going
to happen, Barby, don't worry," Arthur reassured me.

That night I'd barely slept a wink. Every noise, every rustle,
made me think that he was back to take his revenge, and I

tortured myself with thoughts of him doing something to hurt the other animals in my care. I was grateful for my trusty hounds sleeping alongside me, but even so, I felt uneasy for weeks after.

He did reappear a couple of times, but Arthur had taken the wind out of his sails, and I was damn sure I wouldn't give a settled dog back to someone who took drugs. It just wasn't going to happen.

It was a wake-up call, though, and I asked one of my volunteers with a legal background to draw up a contract for anyone leaving their dog or cat with us. I needed to protect both myself and the animal, particularly when an animal is left with us after being mistreated or with people unable to care for them. I included a clause saying that owners could change their minds within a week, to give some leeway, but in this puppy's case, it was totally different. He'd been dumped anonymously, metaphorically thrown on the scrapheap, so I didn't feel any qualms about rehoming him straight away.

It was also a matter of necessity. I knew that if I waited even an extra couple of days, I would be devoted to him, and, however sad it made me feel, I simply didn't have the room for another dog.

"I'm calling him Teddy," I told Diane decisively. I was standing with my back to her, pouring freshly boiled water into a teapot. I carried it over to the table, where I'd placed two cups, the milk and sugar bowl.

"Barby, you need to stop putting four teaspoons of sugar in your tea," laughed Diane in fake shock.

"I like it," I retorted, smiling, as I ladled in the sweet stuff and waited for my friend's response to the name I'd chosen. "Now drink your tea, you deserve it after the work you've done today."

"It is my pleasure," said Diane, waving away my thanks. She was the most trustworthy, hardworking, humble person on my team. She worked like a trooper, always filling in wherever she was needed, on top of her work at the cattery and the FIV area. She really was a marvel, and even though I wasn't the most effusive person, every now and then I liked to remind her how valuable her contribution really was.

"Well, he's as cute and cuddly as a teddy bear, so yes, the name suits him," she said at last, sipping her drink.

"Exactly!" I chuckled. "He's such a softie, and those big paws just make him so clumsy and gorgeous."

We both looked over at him. Teddy stopped chewing on a pretend bone and looked up at us. He was sitting by my feet. He hadn't been more than a few inches away from me in all the time he'd been here.

I reached down to pet him, and as I did so he wagged his tail more eagerly this time, and licked my hand.

"He agrees," I said with a laugh.

Over the few hours Teddy had been with me, he'd already visibly relaxed. He still shook when there were unfamiliar noises, such as the silly cockerels, which were making a racket outside.

"Daft animals," I muttered. "The blimmin' things should crow at 4 am, not 4 pm, but I can't say I'm too unhappy about having a lie-in till 5 am each morning."

"Do you think he'll settle into his new place?" Diane said, looking at the puppy adoringly.

There was just something about this little boy, something that made us all crumble inside. He was a lovely dog, that much was already clear.

"Well, he's only been here a short while, and he's already showing curiosity over his surroundings. He's played with a ball, and explored, which is very brave of him. Yes, you are such a brave boy." Teddy's ears had pricked up and I couldn't help but include him in our conversation.

Outside the trailer, my other dogs were scratching, and barking occasionally, almost as if they were calling out, "Mum, let me in," and "Mum, it's time for my dinner." So far, though, we'd ignored them.

"When Bessie and the others barked earlier, Teddy was petrified. He shrank behind my legs and trembled like a little jelly, but already he's braver, sniffing at the door and trying to get outside. It all bodes well for him moving on. He's even been a bit boisterous. He charged around after a fly earlier and sent quite a few things crashing down. I didn't mind, I'd much rather he was happy than worry about a few books or ornaments."

Diane looked thoughtful. "Just make sure you let his new owners know that he's going to be a very big dog. Wolfhound crosses are renowned for being clumsy and excitable, so they need to be prepared for what they're taking on. He's going to be very loving and affectionate if he's true to his breeding, but that can be a bit much for people. The temperament of the couple needs to fit his rather than the other way round."

At that we both stared down at Teddy. He looked back at us, his dear face looking for all the world like he was smiling at us, his eyes clear and bright. I couldn't resist picking him up, and was gratified when he snuggled into my arms, only shaking a little bit.

Just then, there was the sound of a car driving onto the gravel in the lane.

"That must be them," Diane said.

I felt a sudden swooping sensation in my tummy. They were here already? I wanted to march to the gate and tell them that I wasn't ready, that they should come later, come tomorrow, or not come at all.

"Oh dear, Barby, you are in trouble," I thought as it dawned on me how deeply in love I was with this adorable hound already.

"It's no use you looking at me with those beautiful eyes, Teddy, we need to go and meet these people. I think I'm going to carry you, though. I know you'll only try to follow me otherwise and you might get eaten by Hercules if you try to come on foot." I chattered away at him, trying to make my voice sound jolly even though I felt ghastly at the thought of handing him over to someone else. Somehow, he fitted perfectly under my right arm as I strode across the field with Diane in tow, in my wellies, T-shirt and jeans with their large turn-ups. I had dark blond hair, which I permed into tight curls, and I kept myself in shape through sheer hard work caring for the animals, which meant that even though I was in my mid-forties, I was still a bonny size, weighing almost twelve stone.

Teddy and I crossed the field, and I waved at the couple who were now standing at the metal gate. Both of them looked to be in their early thirties, and they were both beaming at me as I approached. They had a nice car, and were dressed more smartly than I'd have expected for a visit to an animal sanctuary.

"Hello, you're very welcome. I'll just let you through."

With a practiced flick of my left wrist, I unhooked the metal latch and swung the large gate inwards.

"Hello, I'm Alice, and this is my husband, Tom," the woman said, holding out her hand for me to shake.

I shook it rather clumsily with my left hand, the only one that was free, and smiled at her partner. He seemed well groomed in an expensive-looking jumper and shirt, chino trousers and a pair of loafers.

"It's lovely to meet you both. I'm Barby, this is Diane, and this is the fella you've come to see. I've christened him Teddy, which I think suits him perfectly. I hope you like it?" I smiled, holding the enormous pup up a little higher.

"He's gorgeous, what a big boy!" Alice grinned as Teddy wagged his tail enthusiastically, as though already responding to his new name.

"May I stroke him?"

"Of course, though I'd be gentle—he wasn't left here in the nicest way, and of course, as with any rescue animal, we're never sure exactly how a dog will react. We don't get to know their histories, you see, especially those that are abandoned."

"How could anyone abandon you?" Alice crooned, gently stroking his wiry fur.

Her attitude boded well. Tom reached over and started to stroke Teddy too. I was pleased to see both of them reacting to the pup so well.

Teddy's reaction seemed to crystallize the couple's decision. He wagged his tail so hard I almost dropped him as I passed him to Alice. Then it was her turn to gaze up at her husband with that pleading look that I only ever see on a person's face when they've fallen for a pet.

"It seems you're coming home with us, Teddy. My wife has taken a real shine to you, and I can't say I blame her."

I beamed at them both, though inside I felt quite different. My heart felt sore all of a sudden, as if it was empty. I dismissed my feelings. It was best that Teddy moved on to a new home. This couple had rung the sanctuary several times asking for a puppy, and someone had already been to check out their home and their suitability as foster parents to this sweet creature, so really it was just the formalities to go through now.

"I take it you've decided . . ." I said, hesitantly.

"We have. We'll take him," said Alice, her face breaking into a huge smile.

"Well, that's marvelous news. Come with me and we'll do all the paperwork in the trailer. I'd watch where you're walking in those nice shoes though, as it's quite muddy today."

I tried my hardest to keep my tone light. Teddy had a new home. It was for the best.

I walked in front of them, marveling at the people I came into contact with each day: from heroin addicts to professionals like these two, from my volunteers to people from the local rehab and young people with learning difficulties who came every week to help muck out the horses and spend time with Ian, who just happened to be an excellent horse-whisperer. My life and the life of the sanctuary was so varied. At moments like this, I felt real awe for everything my team and I had achieved in this wonderful place. Twilight was just around the corner and I could hear the ducks and geese making their evening sounds, a muted version of their morning cackle. I could hear blackbirds overhead, singing out their territorial stake, making sure other birds kept away as they settled down for the night. I could hear sheep baaing, horses braying and dogs barking before they were fed. It was a good life, and never more so than on spring evenings.

"We have some forms for you to fill in. Nothing too hefty, but we'd like to keep in touch in case any issues arise. You understand that, even though Teddy has been checked over by our vet, we cannot say for sure that he's one hundred per cent healthy or that his behavior is one hundred per cent perfect. Many rescue animals have a hard time settling into a new home, so we encourage all our new owners to be as patient as possible—isolate him in a small room with his toy bone and a blanket, a dog crate would be even better to give him his own special place that he knows is his, and give him plenty of love. You know where we are if anything arises."

As I spoke, both Alice and Tom nodded. They clearly took this seriously, and again, I was pleased at their attitude to taking in an abandoned and possibly traumatized dog.

"I'm looking at my notes, and it looks like we did a site visit a while back to check that your home and garden was suitable for a puppy," I said, flicking through a pile of documents.

"Yes, I think it was Arthur who came out," Tom said, "and he said it was all fine. We have a large garden and a ground-floor flat, and he was happy with us."

Before every rehoming, a member of my team would make an informal visit to prospective owners. Whether it was a cat or a dog that was going to a new place, we always did this as a way of checking out the owners as much as the place where their new pet would be living. We took animal fostering extremely seriously, and I had been known to cancel an adoption on the basis that someone's space wasn't big enough to accommodate an animal that needed space to roam around, or if it was dirty or unkempt. I couldn't bear the thought of sending one of our beloved animals to a home where they wouldn't be taken care of properly.

"If Arthur's checked you out, then we're all good to go. Sign here, and here. Thank you."

The moment had come, and I felt sick. Suddenly I had the mad thought that I couldn't, or wouldn't, let go of Teddy. What was wrong with me? I'd only known this little mutt for five hours; how could I be so tangled up with feelings for this dog already?

"Take him, I can't cope with big goodbyes," I said gruffly. Tears sprang into my eyes, and I wiped them away, embarrassed at my display of emotion. "He's a lovely puppy and he'll make a loving pet. I really do wish you all the best. I just absolutely hate letting any of them go."

"We understand, don't worry," Tom said kindly, reaching out to take Teddy from my arms.

"Come on, Teddy, let's see if we can carry you to the car."

Unhelpfully, Teddy wiggled further down into my embrace, making it impossible for Tom to take hold of him.

"Perhaps I should come to the car with you. Here, take his toy bone. I don't think he's ever had a toy of his own before, so you'd better keep that. Oh, and take this blanket, he's been sitting on it for the last few hours, so it'll smell of him at least." I bustled around, trying hard to keep my emotions in check.

We got to the gate. This time Alice opened it.

Walking to the car, I said a few words of farewell. I couldn't help myself.

"Now then, you be a good boy for your new mummy and daddy. You have to forget the sanctuary, and me, and go and have a nice life. Let's put you onto Alice's lap."

Alice was sitting in the front seat, and she had the blanket spread over her lap. I gently placed Teddy down. He was a bright thing, and as he looked up at me from Alice's lap, it seemed to dawn on him that I wouldn't be coming with him. He started making a heart-rending whimpering sound, scrabbling to return to my arms.

"Now go. I can't say anything else." I turned round, and without a backward glance, I set off back to my trailer. As I walked, I realized I was crying. Bessie, Paddington, Hercules and Wobbly bounded next to me, ready for their food, but my heart was full with only one dog: a scraggly, scruffy, black-haired mutt called Teddy.

Chapter 6

WHO CAN TEDDY TRUST?

Reaching with my toe, I pushed the tap round, sending a surge of hot water into my bath. It was the day after Teddy had been rehomed, and I was lying back in the surprisingly luxurious bathroom of the trailer enjoying some peaceful time and a good soak. I had everything I needed within grabbing distance: my soap, a fluffy towel and a book. The day had been busy, with the kid goats arriving as expected, which had meant we'd had to finish their pens at record speed, alongside performing all the other duties that needed doing each morning and evening, from cleaning out the farm animals to refreshing water butts, carrying out checks, and feeding them all.

I had a sense of deep satisfaction most days, as I knew that every animal on my land would be going to sleep that night with their tummies full and with a place to sleep. Despite that, I was worried about one of the cats in our makeshift hospital.

The cat, a boy named Bunker, had developed a tremor, which was so bad that he often toppled off whatever part of his enclosure he was standing on. We hadn't yet got to the bottom of why he was so stricken, and it bothered me as I suspected that whatever the cause, it wasn't going to be good news.

Bunker had been found at the roadside by a member of the public, and brought to us. We'd failed to discover where he'd come from. With no collar, and no way of identifying his owners, he was a mystery. We'd advertised his arrival everywhere, putting up posters and spreading news by word of mouth, which usually worked, but no one came forward to claim him, and so he became one of our old-timers, living out his days with us. He was a dear thing; a ginger tom with stripes like a tiger running down his back, and a large bushy tail, the tip of which seemed to hover above him as he walked.

Watching him become old and frail was breaking my heart. Every animal here counted, and I'd seen many a grown man— bikers, lorry drivers, builders –weep at the sight of a beloved animal in pain or dying.

I pushed my foot against the top of the tap again and the hot water stopped. At the second sound of movement, Hercules poked his handsome face over the edge of the bath.

"Get down, or you might get wet," I warned with mock severity. Hercules, his big Saint Bernard frame filling most of the space, harrumphed his reply and settled back down, lying on the rug beside me.

Saint Bernards are special dogs. They were bred for the Hospice of the Great St. Bernard pass in Switzerland as working and rescue dogs, pulling stranded travelers from snow drifts. Hercules was tan and white-colored, with a white band across his nose and a big black nose. He sighed as he settled back down, and I could've laughed at his impatience for me to be up and out of my bath.

Just as I dipped my shoulders farther down under the bubbles, I heard a shout: "Barby! BARBY!"

It sounded like Diane. She wasn't prone to hysterics, so something had to be seriously wrong.

"Just as I was enjoying the water," I grumbled, as I bolted up and stepped out of the water, covering Hercules in droplets, which he didn't much like. He got up grumpily and shook himself, spraying me with yet more droplets.

"Get out of my way, Hercules, something's happened," I said in a fluster.

"I'm coming, Diane!" I shouted as I grabbed the nearby towel and roughly dried myself in record time. As I moved, I caught sight of myself in the bathroom mirror. My face was flushed, my blond hair, streaked through with the first hints of gray, was wet against my head. Despite the mess, I had an expression of pure determination on my face. I looked like a woman with a purpose, and that thought made me surprisingly happy. Whatever crisis we were facing, I knew we could overcome it.

"Barby, are you there?" Diane was standing at the trailer door, yelling through to me.

"I'm here, Di, I'm here—what on earth is wrong? Why are you so out of breath, what's happened?" I called back, panicking as I pulled on my boots and strode over to her.

This must be bad, I thought, *for Diane to run all the way across the field.*

"Tell me, where do we need to go? Is an animal in danger?"

Diane was shaking her head. "No, no, it's nothing like that," she panted.

"Well, for goodness sake, tell me, I'm panicking now," I said rather abruptly, my heart thumping.

"You need to come to the entrance, now." Diane's face looked stricken, and immediately my mind assumed the worst. Had another animal been dumped? If so, they must be in a pretty terrible state for Diane to appear so wretched.

"It's Teddy."

My stomach lurched. "What do you mean, it's Teddy? He went yesterday, that's all sorted."

Again, Diane shook her head. "No, it isn't. Barby, he's back."

I took one look at Diane and I sprinted off. I was still young enough to be pretty nifty, legging it across the field to the big gate, Diane hot on my heels. There was Tom, the man who had taken Teddy only the day before, holding the puppy in his arms. From what I could see, the dog looked healthy, and I couldn't see any obvious sign of injury. I'd assumed that something awful must have happened for them to reappear so quickly.

At the first sight of me, Teddy started to wag his tail, though uncertainly.

"What's the matter? Is Teddy okay?" I asked, panicked.

I opened the gate but Tom didn't move.

"Come inside, tell me what's up," I pleaded with him. I couldn't help but feel my heart flip at the sight of Teddy's gorgeous black face and adorable straggly fur.

Tom shook his head.

What on earth was going on?

"I'm sorry but it didn't work out. We—we need to give Teddy back," he stuttered.

I couldn't believe my ears, though to his credit, he looked shame-faced.

"Give him back?" I echoed. "But why? You've only had him for twenty-four hours! That's no time at all to make this decision," I told him, trying to keep my voice steady and keep my rising anger at bay. Did people really think that dogs, especially puppies, were toys or playthings to be picked up and cast off when they felt like it?

"I'm sorry, Barby, it hasn't worked out. Teddy is a lovely dog, very sweet-natured as you said, but he's disruptive."

"What do you mean, disruptive?" I asked, too stunned to be able to do anything but repeat his words. It was true that Teddy had seemed rather clumsy when he spent that few hours with me, but he was a puppy—nothing he'd done in the time I'd spent with him warranted calling him a "disruptive" dog. Perhaps some more extreme behavior had surfaced in his short time with Alice and Tom.

As I stood, trying to figure out what Tom was saying, he suddenly thrust Teddy into my arms, still bundled up in the blanket he'd left in. Instinctively I held my arms out and took the dog. He seemed heavier than I remembered, but he was still trembling.

"I'm really sorry, Barby, we appreciate this isn't ideal, but he chewed up everything in the house, and worse than that, when we came down this morning after he'd cried all night, we found he'd messed inside the house, he hadn't used the litter tray or tried to go outside. We just can't cope with him. He's so big he just knocks things over and it became chaotic very quickly. There's no way we can keep him. We're sorry to have wasted your time." He glanced at Teddy apologetically before turning to leave, his face downcast.

"But you made a donation, we'll need to reimburse you," I said, though I was a little in shock at what he'd said. How could this loving hound have caused so much trouble in just one short night?

"Don't worry about that. We're happy to help. Perhaps next time it'll work out."

Diane, standing beside me in silence, had listened in to the whole exchange. I could see by the look on her face that she was dying to let rip with her thoughts.

I was right. As soon as Tom had got into his car, she let forth a torrent of fury.

"Well, why foster a puppy if you can't cope with a bit of chewing!" she cried indignantly. I had to agree, but I could also sympathize with the shock of introducing a boisterous puppy into a calm household. The couple didn't have children, and so weren't used to any level of discomfort or mess beyond their own. It made sense that having a ten-month-old Irish Wolfhound would've been a radical change.

"Every puppy chews if you don't keep a strict eye on them, and even then, it comes with the territory. And of course he wouldn't use a litter tray if he hasn't been trained to. They knew he hadn't been looked after properly before, so what did they expect? I wonder why they wanted to adopt an animal at all?" Diane finished.

I nodded, but my attention was really focused on the creature still shivering in my arms. He turned his coarse face to me and licked my chin. I could feel his tail wagging inside the blanket.

"Well, thankfully Teddy seems okay so that's the main thing. Let's take him back inside and get him acclimatized to being with us again."

I carried Teddy, my arms beginning to hurt as we crossed the field, the long grass not yet cropped by the sheep or goats as we rotated them in different paddocks throughout the year. There were buttercups flowering, daisies sprinkled through the grasses, and as I walked there was a distinct smell of summertime approaching, with its soft breezes and glorious sun-baked soil.

"You are a lump!" I exclaimed once we'd reached the trailer and I could finally put Teddy down. Predictably, he immediately tried to get back up onto my lap so I sat down on one of my armchairs and he immediately curled up into a ball on my knees, his eyes looking at me dolefully. I couldn't help but chuckle.

"Oh deary, you really are a big puppy, more of a giant pup. I can see they might've found you a bit too much to handle." Teddy looked up at me thoughtfully, his bright eyes shining as though he understood every word.

At times like these, I had to ask myself why people like me run animal sanctuaries, and why people come to us rather than a breeder, their hearts filled with hope, to seek out the animals we rescue. For a sanctuary worker, witnessing the plight of abandoned creatures can be distressing, it is certainly time-consuming, is largely unrewarded and sometimes very difficult work. I did it because I simply couldn't do anything else. My soul, my heart and spirit were bound into this work. But for people like Alice and Tom, nice people who come to us rather than buy a dog from a breeder, what was in it for them?

Every rescue animal was a risk. The dog's background was often uncertain, if not unknowable. The stresses of fostering a dog with dubious or unknown origin, mixed breeding, unknown behavior patterns and diseases was so much harder than picking out a pup from a certified litter. Despite that, people came to us in their hundreds each year to find their companion from the animal detritus left over by our so-called civilized world. Even though things hadn't worked out, I still respected the fact that people like Alice and Tom tried to take in a "difficult" dog rather than take the easy route.

Of course, each time we fostered out a dog they would be checked for mange, disease, ringworm or parasites, and fever, but we never knew for sure if they had a clean bill of health. And yet, every day, I got at least ten phone calls from people interested in the idea of fostering a dog, or wanting to visit the cattery, in the hope of finding their special companion.

At the Barby Keel Animal Sanctuary we had an open-door policy. This meant that we took every animal if it was in our power to do so, regardless of the condition they were in. It meant we never destroyed an animal unless they were in such pain or distress that they had no quality of life. It meant that at any one time, we'd have a cattery hospital full of diabetic cats or very injured or sick felines to care for. We took in diseased dogs, pregnant foals and neglected kittens. We fought for the well-being and happiness of every creature, no matter how bizarre, hurt or abused they were or had been. Our vet bills were out of this world.

The simple answer to the question of why we take them all in is because we love animals. We care deeply about the well-being of all creatures, and the thought of dogs or cats being abused or abandoned makes us rightly very uncomfortable. It is always heartening to see the many adoptions we facilitate, and how even years later, we get updates on how well the animal is doing, and how much love they've brought to people's lives.

There is also another question that perhaps needs to be asked: should we foster?

For some people, perhaps for Alice and Tom, the answer to that question would be a resounding "no." Fostering a puppy brings a whole host of issues and preparations. Puppies are brilliant at disrupting the calm efficiency of a home. A puppy like Teddy is bounding with energy, plus there is the possibility of behavior problems such as chewing, which need addressing. Over the years, I've learnt that the number one reason that people give up dogs, or cats, is for behavioral reasons. The most likely dogs to end up on our doorstep are those who are too energetic, have barking problems, or are prone to biting, chewing or aggression.

Many decisions have to be made before a dog can step one paw inside a new home. If there are already dogs living there, it's necessary to think about how to introduce them to the new arrival. Will the older dogs cope with having a new pup in the house? Does the home have enough space in which a new puppy or dog can play without wrecking the immediate environment? What if the dog is prone to barking? Will it affect neighbors or spouses, children or other animals?

Will the dog sleep inside a crate or basket? Teddy should really have been inside one, and I had been surprised when Tom told me that he hadn't had his own snuggly space to sleep in at night. Dogs are much less likely to foul their area if they have a crate, because they see it as an area that is specifically for them, and therefore want to keep it free of any urine or feces.

It's so important that everyone is on board with a new animal entering a home, and I couldn't help but notice that Alice hadn't been with Tom when he returned Teddy. Perhaps she was the one who'd changed her mind? She'd seemed so keen on the day they met Teddy, but the reality of living with a boisterous, gangly pup creating havoc would've been very different to the fantasy of playing with a small puppy.

It was rare, but we did have fostering failures, and it seemed that Teddy was one of them. I couldn't help but be surprised as his nature was clearly gentle, and he seemed a loving dog with a lovely breed heritage.

Usually, dogs were returned because they hadn't adapted to their new environment. The space may have had challenges: from outside noise, perhaps by being under a flight path or by a busy road. It can also be the result of poor handling by the new owners, and a lack of preparation or commitment to the new resident in their home. Whatever it was, fostering was a hugely emotional, sometimes even turbulent, experience, and it didn't always go well. I understood Diane's anger. She had less patience than me over how people behaved, though she'd snort with laughter if I said that to her face.

"You're an old ratbag, you always have been, and you always will be," she'd say, and I'd have to agree with her. We both took our roles very seriously, and we were always on the side of the animal rather than the human. Yet, as I sat in my lounge with Teddy, stroking the loveable mutt as he sighed and only gave the occasional tremble on my lap, I couldn't help but delight at having him home with me. Somehow he fitted. I couldn't explain it. Sometimes there's a chemistry between owner and pet, human and animal, that is beyond words. It's a pure connection, a kind of symbiosis between two tamed primal animals, and as I recognized it, I realized that letting him go again would be one of the hardest things I'd ever had to do.

"Oh dear, I am in trouble," I whispered, putting my face to his wiry fur and breathing in that familiar, warm doggy smell I loved so much. Teddy sniffed me, sighed again, and laid his head down.

I spoke, making his head tilt up again. "You've been dumped once before, and now you've been 'returned,' which is really another word for being dumped a second time, and here we are, about to look for a third home for you. Will we ever find you a forever home, darling?"

There was no answer to that.

Chapter 7

WHO WANTS TEDDY?

Briiiing, briiiing.

    I held my breath as I waited for the person to answer the phone, for what felt like the hundredth time that day. I hoped against hope that this time the person on the other end would be able to provide the perfect home for Teddy.

"Hello, it's Barby Keel here, calling from the animal sanctuary. Are you still wanting a young dog to foster?

"No? Oh well, then, sorry to bother you, I'm glad you've found a dog, good luck with it all. Bye."

Briing briiiing.

"Oh hello, it's Barby Keel from the animal sanctuary. We have a ten-month-old puppy you might want to come and see— No? Oh, ok, that's fine, shall I take your name off our rehoming list, in that case? Yes, you take care now, thank you."

My heart sank, and with each call, I felt the hope starting to ebb away.

Briiing, briiiing.

"Good morning, it's Barby Keel here, from the . . ."

"Yes, we remember you. Do you have a puppy for us?" The woman on the other end of the phone interrupted me, sounding breathless with excitement.

"Yes, we do, dear, would you like to come and see him? He's an Irish Wolfhound cross with a lovely sweet personality, though he's a bit clumsy and boisterous at times." As I spoke, I glanced over at Teddy who was bounding around the lounge with a stuffed animal, growling and shaking his head, pretending it was his prey. He rolled over, his paws going smack into the cabinet and I saw a china figurine wobble dangerously.

"I must go, but why don't you come up here today, and see if you like the look of him. I warn you, he's a big pup, and he'll grow even bigger . . ."

"That doesn't bother us, we're used to big dogs. Alright, we'll drive up in a couple of hours, once I've spoken to my husband. See you then."

With that, the phone clicked and I replaced the receiver, a huge grin spreading across my face.

"Teddy, it seems like you're in luck. There's an older couple who've wanted a puppy for a while now, and they're coming to see you today. Now, you have to be a good boy when they come, and put your sweetest face on so that they fall in love with you," I said aloud. "Just like I have," I thought to myself, looking at his sweet face.

Teddy pricked up his floppy ears at my words and let out a small bark, his eyes peering out from the tufts of black hair that almost covered his vision. His fur was sticking up at funny angles, some of it looked almost silver in the light, and his mouth that seemed to be permanently smiling.

"Are you getting all gruffly with me," I said, walking over to him.

Instantly, Teddy leapt up and jumped over to me playfully, his tail wagging like mad. He really was such a comical little thing.

"Right, I can play ball with you now that we've hopefully solved the small matter of finding you a home, fingers crossed."

I threw a small chewed ball in Teddy's direction and he sprang onto it, dribbling with it on the rugs laid out across the metal floor.

I felt a huge sense of relief at the thought that we might have found a new owner for this already-beloved creature. There was no greater illustration of how important it was to me than the fact I'd divvied out all my workload for the day to members of my team and volunteers. I'd told them I couldn't do anything until I'd found Teddy the right home.

At 11 am my walkie talkie buzzed.

"Barby, it's Diane. Can we come over for our break now?"

Every day, the volunteers from across the site would traipse into my trailer for their elevenses, squeezing around the kitchen table and spilling onto the sofa and armchairs. It was the only place they could go as the tea rooms were being used in between our Sunday opening times as storage for the tables and chairs that visitors used.

"That's fine, you can all say hello to Teddy," I replied, the radio waves crackling as I spoke.

Five minutes later, my motley crew began to arrive in dribs and drabs. Some took off their wellies and stacked them outside, while others ambled in bringing with them the scent of the warming fields and the animals they were working with.

"The kettle's on," I said, reaching down to scoop up Teddy, who had stopped abruptly when the first volunteer marched in.

"Come on, boy, there's nothing to worry about," I murmured, cuddling him close.

I could feel his little body starting to shake. I looked over at the volunteer who seemed to have frightened him. He was broad-shouldered, in his late thirties, and had dark hair and a stubbly beard.

"Does he remind you of someone . . . ?" I whispered. Teddy was staring at Damian, one of the lads from the local rehab who came in several times a week to help us out. He'd had his struggles with drugs and alcohol but was beating his demons, and was a real credit to the sanctuary. He even showed people round on our Sunday open afternoons, and was gentle with the children who visited. We'd all noticed big changes in him as a result of his time working here, yet something about him seemed to have startled Teddy.

It could be that he reminded the pup of his first owner. It could be that Damian was just an imposing figure, and would have the propensity to startle any young dog. It was impossible to tell.

Teddy whimpered a little, but as the room started to fill up, he settled down on my lap, sitting upright, and watched the hustle and bustle. We had quite a few young volunteers, which always cheered me. It meant that the next generation would be likely to carry on our work. I was always very appreciative of the youngsters in their late teens and early twenties who came to help out. I knew there were so many other distractions in their lives, such as hanging out with their peers, social media and many other things, so the fact they chose to spend their time here, taking care of the animals and doing whatever they could to help, was a godsend.

Finally, Diane trooped in, wearing her trademark bobble hat.

"Oh Diane, good, I wanted to tell you that we might have new owners for Teddy."

"Oh yes, who are they?" Diane wondered, looking thrilled as she poured hot water into a mug. "Do you want a cuppa too?" she added.

"Yes, please, dear. It's that couple who came up here last November looking for a puppy. He's been a bit unwell, which is why they hadn't chased us up. I told them about Teddy and they're very keen."

"Won't he be a bit much for them?" Diane asked, just as Teddy jumped off my lap and went careering off to chase a fly in the lounge area. All at once a small table crashed to the floor, scattering papers everywhere.

"Oh Teddy," I wailed, "what have you done?"

"See what I mean?" Diane chuckled. "He's very, what's the word? Lively . . ."

"All puppies are lively," I pouted, coming swiftly to Teddy's aid. "The whole point of puppies is that they knock things over, make a terrible mess, but are utterly loveable."

"Hear, hear," said Ian as he opened the door. "Your poor neglected other dogs are out there, wanting to come in," he teased.

I gave him my best scowl in response.

"If the wind changes, your face will stay like that," laughed Diane. "Yes, I remember the couple. He was a retired engineer and she was desperate for a new puppy to keep them active. Even so, I still think Teddy might be a bit too high-energy for them."

I thought for a moment, watching Teddy lose his grip on the floor, his big paws sprawling everywhere, his face a picture of utter bemusement. I couldn't take my eyes off him. He really was a tonic, and such a happy little dog deserved a loving home.

"Barby?" Diane interrupted my musings.

"Yes, sorry, dear, I was miles away there. Well, let's see what happens when they come. They said they're used to big dogs so Teddy shouldn't be too much of a shock to them."

A few hours later, I heard the bell by the gate ringing and Arthur, who was passing, let the prospective new owners in. I was watching out for them from my kitchen window.

"Come in, welcome back to the sanctuary," I smiled as I opened the door, leading them inside.

From the lounge came the sound of Teddy giving a few short barks to let them know he was there.

"Is that him?" asked the woman, Jean, who was in her early sixties, with pale red hair and a kind smile.

"It is," I replied, looking over at Teddy proudly.

Teddy stood still and was eyeing everyone warily. I held out a dog treat and he walked over, sniffing the air, and when he gobbled it up, I picked him up.

"He's a bit of a tearaway but such a loving soul. He's going to be big, as he's also got some Briard in him, and he'll need a good walk each day. They are soppy dogs though, very gentle and great family dogs. It is worth mentioning that he isn't toilet-trained yet. Will that be a problem for you both?"

Jean was smiling into Teddy's face while her husband Jim stood back a bit, though he was beaming too. Both of them shook their heads.

"We'll get him trained in no time," Jim said.

"Jim's been rather unwell. His diabetes. . . ." Jean trailed away, looking suddenly upset as she stroked Teddy's black and gray fur.

"I'm sorry to hear that. I wondered why we hadn't seen you at the sanctuary for a while." Jean and Jim had been regular visitors on Sunday afternoons last summer, and it had been noticed when they suddenly stopped coming.

"Now, I must warn you that we have no idea where Teddy came from, as he was dumped here, so we'll never really know his background and history. Is that okay with you? You know that we're here on hand if there are any problems but as far as we can tell, he's a lovely dog and he seems to have survived whatever life he once led very well."

"We've always had rescue dogs so we know what to expect. He is a dear thing, and we've got plenty of space for him to run around and cause chaos!"

Jean giggled. She had definitely warmed to Teddy, and I could see the same expression on Jim's face. Jean and Jim had said they wanted to spend a bit of time with Teddy to make up their minds about him, and so I left them to it, staying close to the trailer in case I was needed.

Half an hour later, Jim poked his head around the trailer door.

"We'll take him. He's a lovely pup and we can train him up, I'm sure of it."

I went back inside, kneeling down as Teddy dashed over to greet me. Picking him up, I couldn't resist planting a kiss on that scruffy head of his, before saying: "Here, why don't you hold him while I fetch the paperwork." I handed Teddy over, and watched with joy as he snuggled into Jean's arms, licking her face excitedly.

I walked over to the cabinet to retrieve the paperwork I needed and glanced back at the three of them. Teddy was sitting with Jean, wagging his tail, and only trembling a little. Jean had bought a new toy with her, a squeaky ball, which he was attempting to chew, while both she and Jim patted and tickled him.

It looks like he's found his forever home, I thought to myself, and felt a lurch of disappointment in my tummy so intense it made me stop in my tracks. *Now, Barby, don't be silly, you can't keep him here, he has to go. Now get on with it, and try not to blub.*

An hour later, after a cup of tea and several signed forms, we were ready for the pup to be taken to his new home. Jean and Jim had signed our release form, saying they accepted full responsibility for Teddy. It also stated that Teddy must remain in their possession and not be transferred, and that they would not object to follow-up visits by an authorized member of the sanctuary. Teddy was now legally theirs.

This time, Teddy let Jim carry him out to their car. After

giving Teddy a brief cuddle, I stood and watched them leave from the door of the trailer. I so hated goodbyes, and I'd already had to do it once with this little pup. I couldn't bear to do it again. My face was streaked with tears as the car pulled away, and I could see Teddy's face peering out of the window from his vantage point on Jean's lap. I caught a last glimpse of them as they turned left up the lane and then they were gone, hidden by the green canopy of trees and thick hedgerows that lined the single-track road.

I couldn't concentrate on anything that day. I shuffled papers, found myself staring into space, then realized that I really did need to get back to work, though my heart felt sore at the loss of Teddy. That evening, as the day settled into twilight, I took Bessie, Hercules, Paddington and Wobbly out for a long walk. The evening was warm, the sun setting late, and insects buzzed around us as we walked. I took the dogs round the back of the horses' paddock, down where the goats and sheep were kept. The land dipped into a valley, and our walk took place against the backdrop of the lush fields and lands of this part of the world. On evenings like this, I couldn't imagine being anywhere else, and I thanked God many times over for giving me this land in this magical place. In winter it was often a different story! Working on the land in the freezing cold or rain, the dark winter skies hanging low overhead, it felt rather more troublesome to live so close to nature.

I skirted round the boundaries of the site and its eight acres, reaching the farm animals and cutting back through, past the cattery and down towards the long faded yellow trailer that was my home, with its television antenna pointing up at a jaunty angle at one end. It wasn't much, but as trailers go, it was bordering on luxurious. Despite its spaciousness, it wasn't a proper home, and for the first time I started to think that perhaps I should live somewhere where I didn't have to catch the leaks with pans each time it rained heavily, or swelter with heat every summer.

The thought passed quickly enough. I had bills to pay and checks to write before I could settle down for the evening. I tore my thoughts back to the present as I let the dogs into the trailer. We had a meeting with the managers and volunteers the next day so I needed to get ready for that. I also had some DEFRA paperwork to do for a flock of unwanted sheep that would find themselves in an abattoir if the sanctuary couldn't rescue them.

With a steaming mug of tea beside me and the dogs flopped out on their bellies, I pulled a pile of paperwork towards me and got to work. I was exhausted once I'd completed my admin tasks but in spite of that, I found that sleep eluded me when I eventually crawled into bed. Every time I closed my eyes, I saw Teddy's sweet face. I hoped fervently that he'd found his forever home but I also felt a kind of grief at having to let him go. Giving away animals was the hardest part of my job, and although I had got used to it over the years, it felt different with Teddy. We had a special bond and he had touched me in a way that was different to the other dogs that passed through my care. Now that the day's work was done, I had plenty of time alone with my thoughts, and all I could think about was his scruffy little face.

* * *

A month later, I was surprised to see Jean and Jim's car pull up outside. I'd just come back in through the gate with my dad and hadn't yet shut it when I heard the crunch of their tires on the gravel.

I waved, hoping it was a social visit, but when Jean got out of the car, her expression told me otherwise and my heart sank.

"Barby, we're used to dogs, we really are, but we've had enough. I'm sorry to do this to you, and we've thought long and hard about whether to keep him, but we've decided we can't." She sighed, wringing her hands.

I'd barely opened my mouth to reply, my head was spinning, when Jim got out of the driver's seat.

"It's a great pity, Barby. We took him in because he's a lovely dog, but it's too much, just too much for us." At that, he looked away.

I couldn't take in what they were saying to me, and stared at them both, looking between their faces, but they both avoided my gaze. I turned to Dad, who stared back at me, his face unreadable, but I knew what he was thinking: "*It's no problem, take the dog back . . . it'll all work out . . .*" Dad was a simple man, a gentle soul, but he knew what was best when it came to animals.

"It's a delicate issue but he won't do his business outside. We've tried to train him to use a litter tray until he got settled, and that didn't work. Then we tried to get him to go outside, but every morning we're greeted by another parcel at the back door and it's simply too much. I can't bear it any longer. He messes inside, then walks it through the house. Sorry, Barby, he has to go."

I could see what it was costing the couple to be so honest, especially about such a difficult matter.

"And he is very boisterous. We thought we could cope, but we've never had a dog as energetic as him. He needs a younger owner who can spend time with him, training him properly and breaking him in. We just can't do it."

Jim opened the boot. Teddy was looking out of a large, expensive-looking dog crate, his eyes staring at me in his doleful way. I almost laughed out loud at the sight of his sweet face peering back at me, but I realized that wouldn't be an appropriate response.

"Oh dear . . ." was all I could say.

Teddy jumped down from the car boot, and Jim handed me his lead. He wore a new leather collar, and it was clear that they'd taken excellent care of him.

"You can keep the lead and the collar. Here's his blanket and toys," Jean added, passing me a plastic carrier bag full of his bits.

"I'm sorry it didn't work out. I'm sure you'll find him a good home soon."

Before I could answer, both were back in the car. I could sense their guilt but was at a loss for words. Teddy and I watched them as they reversed, and then moved away. I looked down at the puppy who was gazing up at me beseechingly.

"You wanted to come home to me, didn't you?"

Teddy wagged his tail, and stood up, licking my hand. I crouched down on the yard floor and cuddled him, feeling tears prick my eyes. This poor dog hadn't done anything wrong in his short little life, and it broke my heart to think that nobody wanted him. As Teddy snuggled against me, his tail wagging enthusiastically, I felt my resolve starting to weaken.

"You're like my little boomerang. Wherever you go, you always come back," I murmured. Teddy responded by enthusiastically licking my face, cheeks and neck.

"Get off, you silly creature!" I laughed, not meaning a word.

As I snuggled into his fur, I couldn't help but wonder what we would do with this gorgeous creature. As I wracked my brains, I suddenly remembered that one of our volunteers had been hoping for a puppy for her son.

I immediately rang her to ask if she had the space for a big dog. She was delighted and agreed to come straight away to take Teddy home for a trial evening. As I waved them off at the gate of the sanctuary, I crossed my fingers that Teddy had finally found a home to call his own. But it was with a now-familiar sinking feeling in my stomach that I saw her car pull back into the sanctuary the next day, Teddy's sweet, furry face peering delightedly out of the window, wagging his tail as though he was delighted to be back.

As I looked into his beautiful dark eyes, something shifted inside me.

Perhaps Teddy had found his forever home after all. Neither of us had expected it, but after the events of the last month, my heart told me that Teddy's true place was right here with me.

Chapter 8

Someone to Love

"Teddy! NO!" I shouted, startled from my work feeding the chickens by the sight of the pup running towards a tiny brand-new chick that had got itself loose in the yard. The tiny ball of yellow fluff was one of Susie the chicken's new brood, hatched a few days earlier, and it was currently stumbling on its spindly legs, cheeping for its mother, unaware of the canine tornado that was fast approaching it.

Teddy flew over, his tail flying, his paws at funny angles, a riot of black fur and gangly motion.

"Teddy, STOP!" I had both hands held to my cheeks. My heart was pounding. *My God he's going to try and eat the chick!*

Diane was standing at the other end nearest the gate with her arms outstretched rather pointlessly. We were both frozen in fear. She'd been trying to shoo the chick towards me so we could catch it and return it to Susie. Teddy had appeared out of nowhere. Diane's face reflected my own shock. She looked up at me as Teddy skidded to a halt, his body seeming to carry on when his paws had stopped moving. He really was an awkward hound.

Everything seemed to moving in slow motion. Teddy opened his large jaws. I reached my arms up, though goodness knows why, but Teddy bent over and scooped the chick into his mouth.

"Noooooo," Diane wailed.

There seemed to be a moment's silence, then Teddy turned and ran to me. I looked at him in pure disgust. He had gobbled up that poor defenseless chick, and he was coming to show me what he'd done.

I opened my mouth to admonish him, then I stopped. Teddy had sat down at my feet and was gazing up at me, his tail wagging. His mouth was perfectly still. There was no gnashing of teeth or swallowing. I realized that the chick must still be alive, and Teddy was waiting for me to do something.

In a state of strange calm, I slowly held my hands out and cupped them together, full of dread at the thought that he might deposit the dead bird into my palms. I almost recoiled, but before I could move, carefully, with absolute concentration, Teddy bent towards my hands, opened his furry great jaws, and gently lowered the little bird into my offered hands.

The chick was alive. It looked rather confused, and was shaking in fear, but it was alive.

"Teddy, you wonderful, wonderful dog. You've saved the chick. You captured it and brought it to me like a real rescue dog." I was beaming at my pup, and in response he wagged his tail so hard he almost fell over.

I looked up at Diane, who had rushed over but kept her distance while this intricate operation was performed.

"My goodness, I've never seen anything like that before in my life. It's a miracle," she said, staring at me with a bemused grin on her face.

"I don't know about a miracle, but I do know that he's a wonderful boy and an absolute treasure, aren't you, Teddy? Aren't you, eh?" As I spoke to him, Teddy rolled onto his back and waved those long legs and giant paws at me.

"I can't give your tummy a stroke now because I've got the chick, you daft dog, but I can find you one of your favorite treats if you come this way."

I walked off, careful not to crush the delicate ball of fluff in my hands. Susie was pecking at the ground in her pen surrounded by the other chicks. I placed the rescued chick on the ground and it immediately made off in pursuit of its mother.

"There you go, Susie, you were missing one."

I crouched there for a moment, soaking in the sight of a busy mother hen with her chicks, one of the ordinary wonders of the world, a familiar sight in farms across the land, yet one that never failed to amaze me. Chickens take just twenty-four hours to make an egg inside their body, and then it takes about twenty-one days of incubation after being hatched for a chick to come into the world. A mere three weeks to create a new life, essentially out of a yolk, was quite miraculous, if you thought about it.

I heard the soft pad of paws on the earth floor. Teddy had

followed me to the pens, but this time I had no fear of him trying to eat one of these little creatures.

"You're such a softie, aren't you, eh, boy?" Teddy nuzzled my hand, licking it finally, before falling back onto his side again, still waiting for that tummy rub I'd promised.

Teddy had been with me for two weeks when he rescued that chick. After the final attempt to try to rehome him with one of the volunteers, it seemed clear that he was meant to live at the sanctuary with me, though I think deep down, I'd known that all along.

The first day with Teddy was heaven. I kept him in the trailer, separate from my other four dogs, with a baby gate at the doorway so that he could see out, and the other dogs could get used to him being around. Whenever a new dog is introduced to a household, it's important to keep them separate so that the new dog can get used to the environment, and any resident hounds can get used to the newcomer.

I was pretty sure that Wobbly, Paddington, Bessie and Hercules wouldn't attack him. They were all good-natured dogs, and had never shown any aggression at all, but I didn't want to take any chances.

Teddy was also an unknown factor. I had watched him to see if he displayed any potentially troublesome behavior, like being ultra-alert to the birds and cats that flew and wandered past occasionally. If he had displayed predatory behavior, I would have worried about his latent personality, but he seemed to show little interest in anything except me and his ball.

I kept a close eye on him for the rest of the day, staying with him inside. I watched each time the older dogs came up to the baby gates, poking their noses through the spaces, trying to check Teddy out.

Hercules was the first to try to make contact. He scented Teddy, bending his head over the gate to try to get a closer look. I held off shooing him away, as I didn't want my involvement to risk any kind of adverse reaction, either Hercules getting defensive or the pup backing off.

Teddy ambled over to see what was happening, sniffing Hercules' outstretched nose. Twilight was falling at the end of another long day, and I knew the older dogs would be tired out from roaming the site, which was always a good time to make new introductions.

"Good boy, Teddy," I said in a low voice as he sniffed at Hercules. It was a good sign that he hadn't tried to lunge or bark at the Saint Bernard, and proved yet again that he truly was a gentle dog.

Hercules soon lost interest and wandered off to sit in the evening's last rays of summer sunshine that were softening over my land. The air was filled with the sound of birds of all descriptions chattering, clucking, cheeping and singing out as the day came to its inevitable close.

Teddy sat by the gate, peering out, looking like a little prisoner staring through the bars, which made me giggle. Wobbly soon appeared, with Bessie and Paddington following. They'd been hovering outside the trailer all afternoon, sensing the newcomer. All three dogs came over to give Teddy a good sniff, and at the sight of three of them, he jumped back a little.

"Don't be scared, Ted," I reassured him. "They won't hurt you, they're just curious."

As I spoke, Teddy's tail started to wag just a little, and he made a few awkward steps forward until he was brave enough to try sniffing the older dogs again. Bessie the corgi wasn't tall enough to peer over the gate, so she had to content herself with pushing her nose as far as it could go through the gaps.

I had to laugh at that. "Bessie, you'll get stuck! Go back, give poor Teddy some space," I chuckled, gently pushing Bessie's face away.

Teddy seemed remarkably comfortable with other grown-up dogs, and I guessed that wherever he'd come from before landing here, he'd been in the company of other dogs quite frequently. Apart from a few, small jitters, he was handling the attention of each different dog with surprising ease.

Sometimes new puppies could become frightened by the unwanted interest, or older dogs could play too roughly and frighten them. By keeping them apart, at least for the first couple of days, was a chance for everyone to become acquainted, and for Teddy to understand that this was his home now.

Any animal fostering comes with huge amounts of change, both for the animal and the human. The human has to adapt to the animal's needs, discover their traits, and spend time and usually need a great deal of patience to make the dog comfortable and settled.

Change is stressful for the dog too. Puppies that have been abandoned or abused, as Teddy had, will often feel confused, frightened and unsure if they will stay in the new place, or be moved on again. Puppies are generally far less open to any new routine or circumstance, and yet this little puppy was breaking the rules. Teddy had spied his ball again and was chasing it rather clumsily in the kitchen, waving his head around and patting it with his paws. He had already demolished several of my cushions, and was eating ravenously, so it was obvious that he was already feeling at home here. In between bouts of frenzied play, Teddy followed me around as I did my chores, changed the bedding, washed up the mugs left by the volunteers during their tea break that day, and tidied papers. Wherever I stepped, he was there, under my feet, and each time I looked down, I saw those sparkly eyes in that doleful scraggy face, and I fell in love all over again.

I'd had to leave the trailer a couple of times to sign for some animal feed, and look after a couple who were coming to choose a cat to rehome.

Each time I left Teddy, his manner changed. Where he was usually a fun-loving, though sometimes anxious puppy, at the sight of me leaving he would curl up and start to cry. Both times, I was only gone for several minutes, but by the time I returned, I could hear his plaintive wails across the field.

"Poor Teddy, did you miss me? Did you think you were being abandoned again? I'd never do that to you, you're my boy now." I gave him a cuddle, and felt his body shake in my arms. I felt terrible but what could I do?

"Separation anxiety. . . . Well, Teddy, it's no surprise. You've been left behind a few times now, and it's to be expected. We'll work through it as time goes on and hopefully help you to get better," I said softly.

That night I kept Teddy in the main lounge which he'd grown used to, with the baby gate between him and my bedroom. That way, I could have my other dogs sleeping in their usual places, sprawled across my bed, or on the floor beside me, ensuring a terrible night's sleep for me, and a lovely one for them.

I placed newspaper all over the floor. Just before I joined the other dogs, I sat with Teddy, telling him how loved he was, and not to be frightened overnight. I showed him the dog flap in the kitchen door and told him what it was used for.

"If you're very brave, you could start by going outside to do your business." I arched my eyebrows at him. So far, Teddy had had a few small accidents, wetting himself accidentally as he played, but nothing more than that.

"Let's see how you cope tonight. We're just in the next room, you won't be alone, though you might feel like it." I patted his rough head and he licked my face.

"Stop kissing me and go to sleep." I said gruffly, smiling down at him.

That night I slept with half an ear cocked, much like one of my hounds, waking each hour or so and straining to hear anything from Teddy.

All night long, I heard nothing. No whimper, no signal that he wanted to go out to do his business, nothing.

At 5 am, Paddington yawned and stretched, waking me from my fitful slumber. Hercules was harrumphing as he did, to show us he was there on the floor, and Bessie jumped up on her short legs and stared at me, while Wobbly slept peacefully by my side. "Alright, alright, it's time for breakfast," I yawned, "let's see how Teddy is."

Then the stench hit me.

"Ah, I think I know already what Teddy's been up to. Okay everyone, get off me, and stay in here."

Teddy greeted me as if I'd been gone for a year. He dashed over, whining, and shaking his tail with so much excitement that the whole of his lower half wagged as well. He tried to jump up and so I shushed him with a hearty "Down, boy," noticing the little trail of piddle he'd left in his joy at seeing me again. I also saw the rather smelly "gift" he'd left me too. He'd messed just about as close to the dog flap as possible, without going outside.

"Why didn't you wake me, eh? I'd have taken you outside," I wrinkled up my nose. Dog poo wasn't the most pleasant thing to be greeted with in the morning, but I was used to cleaning up mess made by any animal, big or small, so it wasn't the end of the world.

"It's to be expected. You haven't been outside properly yet so it was too much to expect that you'd go on your own. Never mind, we'll try again tonight, boy, won't we?" Teddy made a yawn sound that made him look like he was laughing.

"You're too funny to scold. I'll have to get you trained, and quickly, I don't want to wake up to this every morning. At least you did it away from where you were sleeping. We'll get you outside today, on a lead, so you don't bound off, and away from the other dogs for now. Let's get you used to the sights and smells here, and in no time at all you'll have no problem going out at night on your own."

*   *   *

Two weeks later, and nothing had changed. Every morning, I awoke to the familiar smell, even though I'd taken to opening all of my windows. I'd spoken to Dad, asking him if he'd known how to deal with a dog that was resistant to toilet training but he shook his head.

"I don't know what to suggest, Barby, I've never come across a dog like Teddy. There's some sort of psychological block, and you're going to need lots of patience."

I'd nodded, knowing he was right. Patience and tolerance were what was needed, and for this dog, I had them in spades.

Over the days following Teddy's permanent arrival, we'd had a few adventures walking around the land. The first time I took him out, he was wild with nerves and excitement. At first, he'd faltered as he came down the step onto the field. I knew he would be thinking that he was off again, to new people and a new home, because each time he'd gone this way, it was to a different foster home. I deliberately walked the same way, to try and change that connection, walking past the gate where he stopped short. I let him sniff the metal bars for a while, feeling the sun on my back.

"Alright, Barby? How's it going with Teddy?" Ian asked, whistling as strode jauntily across the yard, scattering chickens as he went.

"He's okay, thank you, dear. The main problem is that he's doing his business inside, not even in the litter tray I've had to put down, so I'm trying to acclimatize him to the site so that we can knock it on the head."

Teddy was now tugging at the lead, walking to Ian for a tickle under the chin, which he duly received.

"It takes time, Barby. You don't know where he's come from. He's probably never had any toilet training and so he doesn't understand. Once he realizes he's safe here, I'm sure that'll change," Ian said, his adoration for dogs clear. He was crouching down, his chores forgotten, stroking Teddy's back.

"He's a lovely dog, though, a nice personality. And that's what counts. Most of the other stuff can be taught, but if you've got an aggressive or defensive dog, it can be very difficult," he added.

It was nice to see the affection Teddy was already inspiring in others.

"Right, let's carry on. I want to show Teddy the pigs," I said, starting off, pulling on the lead pulling slightly. It was clear that Teddy was enjoying the attention far too much and was now reluctant to go.

"The pigs, eh? Are you going to see the pigs?" Ian crooned at him, and I burst out laughing.

"Come on, Teddy, or everyone will want you."

We walked past the FIV shelter, and Teddy barely raised a scruffy eyebrow at the sight of twenty or so cats in close confinement.

"You're such a sweetie, what did we do to deserve you, eh?" Teddy gave a small bark, then tried to run off after a bee that had buzzed nearby.

"Stop that, Teddy," I said as I kept walking. Teddy was a ball of energy. He bounced around my trailer, seemingly growing bigger by the day. He was a canine whirlwind, a force of nature but with the gentleness of that chick he saved.

When we got to the pigsties that contained actual pigs,

Teddy stopped in his tracks, stared ahead and cautiously crept up to the wire fencing. He sniffed every part of it that he could, but when one of the pigs decided to waddle up to us, thinking it was food time, Teddy backed off, not taking his eyes off him.

"He's alright, Ted, he won't hurt you. He's just hungry."

The pig's massive snout pushed at the wire, his nostrils flaring as I took out several stale buns I'd saved for him.

I threw them over into the sty, and Teddy and I watched in fascination as he ate them greedily, crumbs flying in all directions.

"At least you don't eat like that," I giggled.

Every day afterwards, I repeated the walk, taking the pup round the site, and each day he seemed to grow in confidence. Yet, despite his obvious happiness, his playful spirit and the cleverness evident in how well he was adapting, each morning I awoke after having no signal from Teddy to find yet another deposit on my floor.

Something had to be done.

Chapter 9

DEVOTION

"**R**ight, now Barby, do you have your overnight bag?" Diane said as I prepared to leave the sanctuary for the hospital.

I'd decided many months previously to have an elective hysterectomy and the date of my operation had finally arrived. It hadn't been an easy decision to make, but I'd had problems in that area of my body, and it felt like the time had come to do something about it.

I hadn't thought much about it, until now, and suddenly I was all of a fluster, packing my stuff, and facing the reality that I'd be away from the site for a full week.

"Erm, I had it here somewhere, dear. Oh look, there it is. Teddy is sitting on it! Come on, Ted, off you come, that's it."

Teddy, who had been with us for just over a month now, reluctantly moved off, then bounced towards the open trailer door. He looked back at me as if he was asking permission to go outside and play, which made me laugh.

"That's it, you go out and play, good dog. Now, Diane, where did I put my glasses? Will you help me hunt for them?"

I was gratified to see how eager Teddy was to run about with my other dogs. He'd only spent two days behind the baby gates before I'd cautiously led him into the field on a lead and let the other dogs chase behind us. I chose the paddock behind my trailer because it was contained by clear fencing. None of the dogs could run too far away, and I would easily be able to spot any signs of trouble.

Then I held him close while Bessie, Hercules, Paddington and Wobbly came over, tails wagging, to sniff each other and make their acquaintance. Hercules lost interest first and wandered off. He was getting to be an old boy now and this energetic pup wasn't of so much interest to him. The other three quickly established a connection, and I'd felt sure enough of all of them to finally let Teddy off the leash after about fifteen minutes of them getting to know each other.

Teddy had bounded away in an instant, though his gait was still awkward as his limbs seemed far too big for his puppy body. Paddington was fast on his heels and Bessie tried to keep up. I could've clapped my hands with joy, seeing them accept each other and get on with the serious business of play. Now and then, Teddy would roll over, kicking his feet up in the air, then bound up and zig-zag across the sweet-smelling field that was overgrown with grass.

There were a few scuffles at first, with some growling and pretend biting, but that was normal for dogs when they played, and I just stood by, not intervening, and letting them get used to each other.

It was clear to me now that Teddy had grown up with other dogs around him. Perhaps he was owned by a breeder who tired of his boisterous nature and his ability to create havoc wherever he went, or perhaps it was the issue of his lack of toilet-training, something that still eluded Teddy, no matter how many times I took him out each day and told him to "do your business." Each morning, I still awoke to a parcel left by him inside. I wasn't too bothered, even though it had been going on for a while. I reasoned that once he was properly adjusted to being here, and accepted by my dogs, it would change.

How wrong I was.

"Diane, we need to put the goats on my paddock while I'm away, the grass is becoming like a forest."

"Don't worry, Barby, it's all in hand," Diane said, smiling. She had my bag in one hand and my glasses in the other.

"And you will take care of Teddy, and the others . . ." I asked anxiously. I knew very well that Diane would look after Teddy as if he was her own, but I was certain that Teddy would miss me. His separation anxiety was something that had really shown itself the first time I left him with Diane to go to my weekly darts match. I was an avid darts player and had won many trophies over the years, and it was a passion of mine that almost rivaled my love of animals. My nights out in Sidley with my two darts teams were treasured time that allowed me to indulge in my hobby, and even with Teddy to care for, I couldn't let them drop.

The first night I went out, I'd asked Diane to dog-sit Ted in the trailer. She'd arrived, and was greeted joyously by

Teddy, who was a delight, a friendly, happy ball of energy. Everything changed when I picked up my jacket and nodded to Diane that I was on my way.

Teddy's ears pricked up. He tried to rush over to me, expecting to go out with me, but Diane held him close. I took a last look at him, and shut the trailer door behind me, heading out to my Tuesday night match with my team The Home Guard, which I'd played with for a good many years. As I walked away, a wail from Teddy rang out that seemed to penetrate my bones and stopped me in my tracks. It was one of the most heartbreaking sounds I'd ever heard.

I found it hard to put one foot in front of the other, it was so distressing, and at one point I even stumbled. I knew I had to break the cycle with Teddy and teach him that he could trust that I would come home to him each night, but I knew that right now, my beloved hound thought he was being abandoned again.

I was barely able to concentrate on the match that evening, and as a result we suffered a rare loss.

"Everything alright, Barby?" asked Chris, a handyman who had recently started doing some construction work at the shelter.

"I can't stop thinking of Teddy. He howled like a beast in pain this evening as I left and I felt really awful at leaving him. Poor Diane will have had a terrible time trying to calm him down. He follows me everywhere, he's very attached, and of course, he's been abandoned so many times now that he's expecting it each time I leave him, even for a couple of hours," I replied sadly.

"Don't worry, Barby, if anyone knows how to help him, it's you," said Chris reassuringly. He was a nice chap, and I trusted him enough to tell him how I felt. I wasn't usually so open about my feelings, preferring to keep myself to myself, only letting my guard down when an animal was in trouble.

I shrugged. No one on earth could take away the fear and pain Teddy had suffered in his life, yet most of the time now he was a well-adjusted, happy dog; it was just separation that brought up those anxieties.

"From now on, I think I need to start leaving him with Diane for an hour every evening to teach him that I'll always return. Otherwise, goodness knows how he'll cope when I go in to be spayed," I sighed.

"Spayed? What on earth are you on about?" Chris laughed.

"Oh, my hysterectomy, sorry, I call it being spayed as we all know I'm more animal than human," I laughed.

It was true though. When I'd agreed to have the operation, I hadn't had Teddy, and my other four dogs were fine to be left in the capable hands of Diane and Ian. Things were different now though, and I wondered how on earth Teddy would cope without me.

"Right, I can't put it off any longer. I have to go or I'll be late to get on the ward," I said stoutly, though inside I didn't feel nearly as strong as I sounded. I was as heartbroken as Teddy would be at the thought of us being parted for a whole week. Would he still remember me? Would he accept me back if he thought I'd abandoned him forever?

After the disastrous first evening away from Teddy, I did

what I'd said, leaving Teddy alone with Diane for a short while to get him used to my absence. Every evening, I'd pretend to go out, and Diane held onto Teddy. I'd then go for a big walk around the edges of the site, checking in with Arthur or one of the other volunteers as I went, following the progress and frustrations of each day in close detail. Once I'd done a circuit of the land, I'd head back to find Teddy wild with joy at seeing me, his tail flailing about, his clumsy paws jumping up, trying to lick my face as I bent down to stroke him. Each day, the wailing had reduced until the last night, the day before I was leaving for my op, when there'd barely been a peep out of him.

"Let's hope he's cured of his separation anxiety now. You mustn't worry about him. Whatever happens, I'll take proper care of him, you know that," Diane said. "And preparations for the Summer Fair Open Day are all in hand, so don't worry about that either."

Every year in August we held a fundraising day, like a village fete, at the sanctuary. It was two months away, but already we'd started making plans for the different stalls, while each morning I spent a few hours ringing around local businesses and charities asking for donations for our prize raffle. Each year we were given some wonderful gifts—bottles of good wine, free trips and plenty of smaller items—and it always helped us raise enough money to cover almost half of our annual running costs, a sum that generally ran into the thousands of pounds.

"Yes, thank you, Diane, and don't forget to call the people on the list I've made, and ask Arthur to repair the fence at the bottom of the sheep paddock as it's looking wonky—oh and the cat hospital needs a new refrigerator to store the medicine. . . ." Once I'd started to list everything that needed doing, I found I couldn't stop.

"Just go, Barby," Diane said abruptly.

I stopped. She was right.

Minutes later I was inside my ex-partner Les's car being driven to Eastbourne Hospital. Les had kindly volunteered to take me as we were still in touch. I realized, as I sat there for the short drive, that I was a little scared of the procedure I was about to undergo, but despite this, or perhaps to make light of it, I'd refused to stop saying I was being spayed.

"It's okay, I'll take it from here," I said to Les as we arrived.

"Are you sure you don't want me to come in with you?" he asked.

"I'm sure. I'm perfectly capable of walking myself to the ward," I grinned in response.

"Right you are, Barby," he chuckled. He knew me well enough by now not to argue with me! As he drove off, I turned to the glass doors at the hospital entrance. I walked in, past the patients sitting outside, some attached to drips on poles, some just in their gowns enjoying the sunshine.

"It's Barby Keel," I said to the receptionist, "I'm due in for an operation."

I didn't return home for eight days in the end.

By the time Les came to pick me up, I was thoroughly fed up of being stuck in a ward with machines bleeping at my sides, and drips feeding into various veins on my arms. I'd had a steady stream of visitors, and everyone who'd come had been quizzed first-and-foremost about Teddy.

"How is he?"

"Is he missing me?"

"Is he eating properly?"

"Has he used the dog flap yet?"

My questions went on and on, and I couldn't wait to get home.

I grumbled as Les pushed me in a wheelchair through the hospital's gleaming corridors and out to his car.

"They tell me I've got to rest for a month! A month? Can you imagine? I've never rested in my life. I've got people to call, the hay bales to organize—do these doctors think that we have no lives of our own?"

Les ignored me, as per usual.

"Stop worrying, you old bag, we'll do everything that needs doing. You'll just have to sit on your throne and give us your orders, Your Majesty."

I giggled at that.

"Well, I might quite like that. In any case, I can't do any lifting for the next six weeks, so I won't be lugging sacks of animal feed around, that's for sure."

As the car drew near to Bexhill, I breathed a sigh of relief. I was in some discomfort but I didn't care as long as I could get home to my animals.

"Now, we have to be a bit careful as Teddy will go wild when he sees you," Les warned as he indicated to turn left into our lane.

"How do you know that?" I asked rather grumpily. "He may have forgotten about me altogether. Don't forget he's used to being dumped and left. He might think that I've abandoned him for good . . ."

As I spoke, I felt a lump in my throat. *Don't start crying, Barby, pull yourself together* . . . I admonished myself, though the lump remained firmly in place. I felt heartsick at the thought that Teddy might not remember me, or might be so hurt by me leaving that he preferred Diane's company now. My face must've looked a picture of sadness because Les laughed as he glanced at me, shaking his head.

We were heading down the winding one-vehicle-width lane that lead down the valley and into the sanctuary. I smiled at the familiar sights, the large houses dotted along the roadside, the overgrown hedgerows that meant Les had to crawl along, beeping his horn every now and then to warn anyone approaching from the other direction.

The air smelled warm, like honey, and there was the distant sound of horses braying in another field.

"Do you seriously think that that daft dog would choose anyone rather than you?" Les teased.

"How can you be so sure that he hasn't transferred his affections? It happens when a dog is fostered out, so why not now?"

"Just wait and see," Les said mysteriously.

We pulled into the driveway, past the sign saying Barby Keel Animal Sanctuary, past the sties where the dogs were housed on our right, fenced off from view. There was a large garden run created for dogs that might be too predatory or aggressive to be rehomed to anyone but a dog specialist. It was unoccupied now, but I barely noticed it, for something had caught my eye.

Behind the large metal gate was a black figure, a rather large, straggly, scruffy-looking black dog, which had jumped up onto his hind legs as the car drew up.

"It can't be . . ." I said, a huge smile breaking out on my face.

"It is," replied Les. "He's been here every day, pining for you at the gate. We didn't want to tell you in case it upset you, but that's how much he's missed you."

I couldn't wait to get out but I had to be patient as I could only hobble a few meters without help. Les came round and opened the passenger door for me. I gripped his arm and made my first faltering steps back home.

"What a good boy, Teddy, you're such a good boy," I said before I was even through the gate, and at the sound of my voice, Teddy could hardly contain himself. He jumped and jumped, his whole bottom end wagging as well as his tail. He made a kind of joyful whimpering sound and ran around in circles, making Diane, who was approaching from my field, laugh at the sight of him.

"Welcome home, Barby, how are you feeling?"

Diane laughed as I grimaced. "That bad, eh? Well someone's missed you, in case you couldn't tell!"

"You'll have to keep hold of him as he might knock me over. I'm a bit of a frail old lady today," I said.

"Nonsense, you've never been frail in your life, Barby, but you're right, I think we do need to calm him down so that he doesn't risk hurting you in his excitement. He's shown utter devotion though. From the day you left for hospital, he's waited by the gate, waiting for you to return."

My heart swelled as I heard this.

Les opened the gate and I hobbled through. It had never felt so good to have my feet planted firmly on my land. I bent over and Teddy, though being held by his collar, showered me in kisses, while I held his face and kissed his funny wiry fur, which tickled my face.

He had grown even bigger. He was now almost a year old, and the only signs he was still a pup were in the bulky blundering movements he made, and the mismatched size of his paws relative to his gangly legs. To my mind he was utterly beautiful.

Teddy bounced and ran in circles of joy all the way back to the trailer, where Diane had set me up with a chair and rug in the shade.

"Right, madam, there's no work for you today, your job is to relax and sit with Teddy."

"Hang on . . ." I objected, but Diane butted in with: "Listen, Barby, I know you're strong and very feisty, but these are doctor's orders. You have to rest and let your body recover or you won't be well enough for the Summer Fair. Are you listening?"

I nodded rather ungraciously.

I'm a doer. I like to be busy all the time. Goodness knows how I was ever going to learn to relax.

"Tomorrow we'll sit together and make a list of everything that needs doing, and you can learn the art of delegation."

Diane looked at me, her kind face beaming. She was a caring soul, and one of my most trusted friends. She was always there to help anyone in need, and I valued her advice, so I nodded again. This time with much more grace, and with gratitude.

"Thank you, dear. Now Teddy, stop trying to get on my lap. You're too big anyway and everything's a bit ouchy."

I pushed him away, feeling my insides twinge with pain. "Will you pass me my bag, dear? My painkillers are long overdue. Thought I could do without them . . ." I admitted, making Diane shake her head at me.

She went back to the kitchen and brought out a glass of water and a cup of tea.

"There are four sugars in there to give you a boost. Take your pills and enjoy sitting with Teddy," she ordered.

"Oh, and we had a couple of calls while you were away, people looking for a puppy to foster."

"You can tell them we don't have one. Teddy is my dog, and always will be. He's staying here at the sanctuary and that's that."

Chapter 10

WORK BEGINS

"Oh Teddy, still leaving me a little present each morning, are we? What on earth are we going to do with you, eh?"

I scooped up the mess and opened the trailer door to let the new day in. I was still hobbling a little but I'd been good and I'd rested, and my operation scars had healed beautifully over the previous few weeks.

It was a sunny July morning and Teddy had been living at the animal sanctuary for two months now—with no progress whatsoever with his overnight problem.

I'd decided that the only logical explanation was that he was scared of using a dog flap. Watching him in the cabin, I had a sudden eureka moment. As soon as I was feeling well enough to get down on all fours, I decided that I was going to show him how to use it myself. I reasoned that he'd probably never seen one before, so for days on end, I'd crouched by the flap, opening it little by little so he could poke his hairy nose outside to get the process started.

I put treats just by the entrance, enticing him to get close before luring him through it. Teddy appeared to have no problem sniffing round it, then wolfing down the treats, so with some effort and a few swear words, I managed to get down onto my hands and knees and hovered at the opening.

"I hope you realize what a sacrifice to my dignity I'm making for you, Teddy," I sighed.

Teddy was still chewing on a treat, taking no notice of me at all.

"Oi, you, Teddy, look at me, look at Mummy . . ." I started to shuffle through, poking my head out and probably looking pretty comical in the process.

"I knew you were more dog than human," shouted Arthur, who had chosen that exact moment to pass by with a wheelbarrow filled of hay.

"Yes, well, I wish I was a dog rather than a human sometimes," I shot back, making him smile.

"Come on, Barby, you can get through. Come on, girl . . ." Ian had joined him. He looked like he'd just got here. Both men were wearing ripped shorts, dirty T-shirts, baseball-style caps and huge working boots. They were standing in the field, side-by-side, their arms folded, watching me with huge grins on their face. Apparently, I was the funniest thing happening on the site that day.

"You can both stop smirking," I bellowed. "I'm trying to teach Teddy to use this blasted dog flap. He's still messing inside, and it's driving me mad. Now it's summer, the smell is terrible."

"He won't use the dog flap? Why?" Ian asked curiously.

"That's what I'm trying to find out. It's impossible, I've spent hours showing him what to do, opening it, leaving treats outside but he shows no interest at all."

Just as I was finishing my sentence, I felt something large and hairy push past me, and a great black tail whacked me in the face.

"Teddy!"

The pup had brushed past me and walked straight through the dog flap as if he used it every day.

"Well, thank goodness for that," I exclaimed. It seemed my problem was now solved.

Meanwhile, Ian and Arthur had dissolved into fits of giggles.

"Come on, Barby, I want to see you climb through it. I'll give you a treat if you do," Ian called.

"Bloody men," I muttered under my breath, shielding my eyes from the sun with my free hand. The other was keeping me upright as I leaned through the door.

"What was that Barby? We didn't hear you!" Ian was trying not to laugh.

"Bloody men!" I shouted this time, making both of them howl with laughter.

I backtracked into my kitchen, and got up, brushing myself down.

"Haven't you both got work to do?" I barked, pretending to be cross with them.

Both men were loyal team members, and were absolutely committed to helping each and every animal on the site, even though they could both be quite grumpy at times. I valued their knowledge, but it didn't mean I couldn't join in the joke.

"Yes, Barby," they chorused, neither of them moving an inch.

Teddy had run up to them and was now being petted and patted by both men.

"Well, you'd better get on with it then," I cackled. "Come on, Teddy, it's breakfast time."

At the sound of my voice, the scruffy mutt ran hell-for-leather towards me, his tongue lolling out of his mouth, his tail going round in a kind of circular motion. As he leapt up to kiss me, I almost fell flat on my back. He was turning into a big dog, and of course, he had no idea how large he really was. He sent my mug of tea flying, the hot liquid missing him by inches, and the china broke into pieces on the floor.

"Oh Teddy," I sighed, "what am I going to do with you, you great lump?" I didn't mean a word, though. My adoration for the beautiful creature seemed to grow each day.

That night, I didn't bother putting down the newspaper sheets on the floor as I'd done each evening since Teddy arrived. Now that I'd taught him how to use the dog flap, I was confident that I had finally cracked the issue.

Wrong again.

The next morning, I awoke to the mess Teddy had made overnight.

I couldn't be cross with Teddy. There was clearly something that had happened to him in his past or something amiss somewhere if he couldn't perform the simple act of doing his business outside. That much was obvious, but what on earth was it?

* * *

Many dogs that come into rescue shelters come with behavioral issues like excessive barking, a constant need to try
and escape, or without toilet-training.

Their actions might have been the reason the dog was
dumped or left at the sanctuary, or they might've developed
as a result of being given away. Either way, it was up to my
team to put right whatever they could to ensure a dog is able
to be given a new, permanent home.

Some dogs arrive in a state of fear, which creates the stimulus for alarm barking. This is the kind of behavior that saves
the inhabitants of burning houses, but it can also be a nuisance
when it's triggered by almost anything in the immediate environment, from dogs on the television to people walking by
the window, or the arrival of the postman. In this scenario we
know to reduce the stimulus by keeping the dog somewhere
quiet and building up its confidence over the days, weeks or
months that it's with us.

Dogs can also have temper tantrums, much like young children. They can bark uncontrollably as a way of getting that
treat, or that extra walk, or they can simply feel bored if they
aren't given the chance to socialize with other animals and humans. Being kept in a kennel or yard with no distractions can
be distressing, and we make sure to give those hounds plenty
of love and stimulation to offset any earlier conditioning.

Some dogs become strays and end up at our door because
they are adept at escaping from anywhere, whether by jumping over walls, wiggling through a hole in a fence or even digging under it. In cases like this, they need to be kept secure

until they can trust that where they are in a safe and loving space.

Toilet-training, or lack thereof, has always been one of the main reasons for people giving up their pets. Some dogs simply resist the whole process, and if someone hasn't got the time to spend teaching an animal, and to clean up their mess, it's easy to see why they might want to give up their pet.

House-training is vital, and yet it does take time. Since Teddy had arrived in spring, I'd taken him out on the hour, every hour, to try and make the connection between doing his business and the outdoors. Each accident often felt like a huge setback because it reinforced the behavior rather than solved it. Putting a puppy in a crate or confining it overnight, like I'd done with Teddy, was supposed to make it easier to hear when the dog needed to go to the toilet, and would be the signal for the owner to get up and take them out.

Teddy simply wouldn't do it. He had never given me signals during the night that he wanted to go out, and he had refused to use the dog flap, even now, when I'd established that he could use the opening perfectly well.

I just couldn't understand it. It was a mystery I obsessively mulled over while I recovered from my operation.

I consulted Ian, who was our resident expert in canine behaviour, but he was stumped too. I talked to everyone on the site, hoping for a solution, but no one had any answers.

I started putting dog treats outside the dog flap at night, trying to tempt Teddy out, but each morning was the same: the treats lay untouched and the dog flap unused.

"What I don't understand is that Teddy is not an unintelligent dog. He adapted really well to Bessie, Hercules, Paddington and Wobbly, and to being here with all the strangeness of the animals and the land. So why would he consistently not do this one thing? What is he scared of?"

Diane shook her head.

"You've tried everything, Barby, I just don't know what the answer is."

We were sitting on some garden chairs in the area beside the trailer, watching the last of the sun's rays depart. The geese were getting excited about something over by the yard, and we could hear the birds in the nearby line of ash trees to the north-west of the entrance as they performed their evening song. It should've been a perfect evening but I couldn't stop worrying about Teddy.

"It can't go on, Di. I can't cope with the sight and smell of Teddy's presents each morning. Something has to change or I'll have to accept he can't live with me in there. There isn't enough space as it is, without having that to contend with," I said, sadly. I hated feeling unable to help an animal, and I'd grown so fond of Ted that the thought of him living on another part of the site was heartbreaking.

"Well, I think you should build an extension on the side of the trailer anyway. Teddy is massive now, and he's growing by the hour, or so it seems. Soon you won't have room to swing a cat, let alone have five dogs in there. You should add an extra room, ask Ian and the boys to build it, then see how Teddy is doing once you've got a bit more space," Diane said. She always had a practical solution, and even if it wouldn't solve the main problem, the thought of having a bit more room was an attractive prospect.

"Yes, that's a good idea. I'll ask him tomorrow, thank you, dear."

At that moment, all five dogs appeared from the dip in the valley, which led the fields away and out of sight. They were running towards us, a picture of healthy, happy dogs. I sighed with contentment as Teddy nuzzled against my leg, desperate to be caressed and tickled.

"Teddy, I have no idea what happened to you in your first ten months of life that means you can't behave like a normal dog, but I'm determined to solve this problem, do you hear me?"

As though in response, he licked my nose, making me laugh.

"Tonight, you'll come in with me and the other dogs, and perhaps you'll follow their lead and let them take you outside when it's toilet time? Yes?" Teddy licked my cheek this time.

"Oh, that's a definite 'yes,'" laughed Diane.

Overnight, I tried to sleep in the tiny leftover sliver of my own bed that I was lucky to be given by my dogs. Teddy slept right next to me, his face almost touching mine, while Bessie curled up at my feet, Wobbly sprawled horizontally across the center of the bed, making me creep to the edge, and Paddington and Hercules slept on the floor.

I woke frequently through the long hours, as the dogs twitched and growled in their dreams. I didn't mind—my love for them went far beyond owner and pet. They were more like children to me, and even though I had Teddy's face breathing next to mine, Wobbly's feet digging into my side and Bessie lying where my feet should be, I was happy enough.

It made no difference. I'd been aware of both Wobbly and Bessie getting up and going out overnight, but I hadn't heard a peep from Teddy and I'd dozed most of the night, yet had missed him getting up and repeating the same thing. I was so disappointed when I did finally rouse myself that I could've wept. I loved Teddy, but I knew this couldn't go on.

Later, I spoke to Ian about adding an extension, and in no time at all, it seemed, the building of my extension was underway. I watched the team lugging wooden stakes and bricks over to the trailer, but my heart had sunk to my boots. If Teddy didn't improve, if he didn't get this right and start doing what he should be doing, then I couldn't see how I could keep him with me. He'd have to go and live in the kennels. Having him living with me in the trailer in his current state was unsanitary and unpleasant, and as I still wasn't feeling great in myself, I found the daily removal of his mess a grind and immensely dispiriting.

I knew that dogs were rehomed for much less, but never once did it cross my mind to give him up completely. He would stay at the sanctuary no matter what happened or didn't happen, but if he moved into the kennels, I knew he wouldn't be exclusively mine, he wouldn't live with me, and that thought made my heart feel heavy.

Chapter 11

Peter's Visit

"Barby, it's Peter on the phone for you." Diane called over to me as I sat sunning myself, and writing out checks.

"These vets bills go up every month . . . we need to raise a hell of a lot of money next month. We need to start advertising the Summer Fair as its only weeks away and at this rate we'll never get everything done, let alone get enough people in to help . . ." I was deep in concentration, muttering away to myself as I dealt with the mountain of paperwork.

"Barby, can you hear me?" Diane walked towards me holding my mobile.

"What was that, dear? Sorry, I was concentrating," I replied, still not giving my friend my full attention.

"Worrying more like, if I know you," Diane admonished. "Your brother is on the phone for you. Or are you too busy *concentrating* to take it?"

"I'm never too busy doing anything to not speak to Peter," I said rather sniffily, holding out my right hand for the phone.

"You can forget the attitude, madam," Diane laughed.

I stuck my tongue out at her, a gesture I used to do to my older brother plenty of times as a child.

"Peter dearest, how are you?" I asked, leaning back in my chair. I was overjoyed to hear his voice. We didn't speak that often these days as we were both busy people, but when we did talk it didn't matter at all, and we were soon chatting away as if no time at all had passed since the last time we'd spoken.

"Barby, can I come and see you? I've got some news for you," he said. His voice was deeper than mine but it had the same hint of Sussex twang to it.

"Of course you can, you can meet my new pup, Teddy," I replied, delighted that Peter was coming. We hadn't seen each other for ages, maybe months, even though he lived in Eastbourne, so this was a rare treat.

If there was any catch to his voice, I didn't hear it. There was nothing to suggest that there was anything different about his manner. I've often thought back to that brief conversation and wondered whether I could've known, somehow intuited that something was terribly wrong.

I was so pleased to hear from him, I don't think I even asked him what it was he needed to tell me, except to add: "Oh, and don't be bringing me bad news, we've had enough of that. One of our cats had to be put down yesterday, and two chickens have died of old age."

Peter was silent for a moment, then he said: "Don't worry Barby, I'll be over tomorrow. Does that suit you?"

"Of course it does, I'll have Diane pick us up some cake from Sidley. See you then, bye."

I put the phone down, oblivious to anything but the delight

I felt at seeing the brother who'd appeared two years earlier than me, though he wasn't the firstborn. Mum had lost the first baby, a boy, and somehow, I always felt that when I came along, the grief over the loss of her firstborn came tumbling out and created the coldness she felt towards me. I was born a twin, born second to a girl who didn't last more than ten minutes. Mother always said I'd pushed her out in a fit of temper, and deep down, I think somehow she always blamed me for her death. On top of that, it sometimes felt as if, in her mind, I could never be as good as that boy who didn't live. I think she felt that I was a poor substitute, a scowling, skinny, filthy ragamuffin who ran wild, blew raspberries at authority (especially her) and gave all my love and devotion to Dad and his strays. She felt the loss of my twin sister keenly, and all that emotion, grief and anger was directed at me, the surviving twin, the one she just couldn't bring herself to love.

Peter, on the other hand, was the object of her devotion. He was a sunny child, and with his golden hair, blue eyes and sweet personality, he could do no wrong.

We spent many nights hiding in the crude Anderson shelter in our back garden, waiting for the bombs to stop falling during the war with Granny Grunt and Grandpa Whiskers, my mother's parents.

I was six and Peter was eight when we were evacuated with our mother to a farm in deepest Gloucestershire.

"That's my gas mask!"

"No, that one's mine, this smelly old one is yours," I sneered at my brother as the train pulled out of Eastbourne Station. I think underneath my bravado, I was petrified of leaving everything I knew, our terraced house in Firle Road, my grandparents and beloved father, to head out into the countryside, a place that really did feel like darkest Peru.

"No, it's mine, Barby," said Peter with dignity, "but as you want it so badly, it's yours."

Well, I hadn't known what to say to that.

My mother did.

"Tsk, tsk, Barbara"—she always called me by my full name, a name I hated and have never allowed anyone to call me since— "why can't you be more like Peter, and less . . . less . . . argumentative." She put great emphasis on the last word, as if somehow, by magic, she could transform me into a golden-haired, pleasant, smiling child instead of the ratbag I really was.

I stuck my tongue out at my brother, but he only grinned.

I looked at Mother darkly. She was a stout, plain-looking woman with deep lines of disappointment on her face, a short brown bob, and she always wore a faded apron, the kind that washerwomen wore.

She wasn't a kind woman, except to Peter, yet, unlike many siblings given the dregs of a parent's affections, I refused to hate him. I was as besotted by my brother as she was, and we were as thick as thieves together, which might also have been a reason she didn't appear to like me. I sometimes wonder now if she was jealous of mine and Peter's closeness.

I saved his life only a few weeks later, when a German bomber had tried to use us as target practice as we played in a field. I'd screamed at him to dive into a haystack, as the roar of the plane and the rat-a-tat-tat of the machine guns clattered overhead. Thankfully the Luftwaffe missed us, but it was an experience so intense it made our bond unbreakable. Even now, fifty years later, I had dreams of that bomber circling overhead, desperately looking for somewhere to run to, the two of us diving inside the haystack, panting, pressed close inside a mess of prickly hay, the sweet smell suffocating me, sharp, pointed strands sticking into me as my heart thumped, thumped, thumped, until the aircraft drone moved off and we both let out a sigh of relief.

Seeing Peter scrambling out from his hiding place, covered in bits of straw, his face bright red from almost suffocating inside the hot dark uncomfortable innards of a haystack, made me suddenly collapse into fits of laughter. He took a long look at me too. I must have looked the same, like a scarecrow gone wrong, and he too was soon gasping for air in between howls of relieved laughter. To this day, I don't think I've ever laughed as much as that, ever enjoyed a moment so purely and so freely.

My adoration for my brother had only increased from that moment, and my treatment from my mother, that cold-hearted, sour-faced woman, rolled off me, like droplets of rain from one of my ducks' backs.

Teddy's paw touching my knee brought me slap bang back to reality.

"Sorry, Teddy, I was miles away, remembering old times with Peter. You're going to meet him tomorrow, how exciting. We'll have to give you a bit of a comb and brush, maybe even a bath, so you're looking like a smart boy."

Teddy cocked his head to one side as he often did when I

spoke to him. His dear not-so-little face looked for all the world like he understood and was nodding along.

I laughed. "Come on boy, let's go and get you smartened up."

As I stood up, Teddy was immediately by my side, his body reaching up almost to my waist now. He was growing so big.

I led him through to the bathroom and helped him clamber into the tub, and proceeded to wash him in my bath. He was good as gold, and only objected when it came to getting him out and toweling him down. He took objection to that, and leapt out, his face a picture of affront, and instead of letting me pat him down, vigorously shook himself from the tip of his nose to the end of his tail, spraying me and everything within a two-meter radius with water.

"Teddy!" I exclaimed, tutting at him as the water soaked me, though I could never truly tell him off; he was far too loveable for that.

The next day, I awoke early, excited about Peter's visit. I was so looking forward to it that I didn't even tut over Teddy's continual messing inside the trailer. The "extension" was finished now, and had been built to house Teddy, so at least the mess was out of sight to some extent, but I still hadn't cracked the problem, and I was at a loss as to what to try next. I had run out of ideas.

"Never mind, let's not think about that today, eh, Teddy? We'll think about my brother coming instead and I'll take a day off from worrying about what to do with you."

Teddy wagged his hairy black tail, and looked at me with those daft smiling eyes, before his gaze alighted on a butterfly that was flitting past. He shot off, jumping up to try and reach it, and in his haste, sent my bowl of cereal flying.

"Teddy," I grimaced. I wasn't going to get cross today though. I wanted Peter to see me in a good mood.

I was waiting over by the gate when his car finally pulled into the driveway. I opened it and walked out to greet him, beaming as he approached.

"He looks a bit thinner, though it suits him," I thought to myself as I finally caught sight of the fifty-eight-year-old Peter, a bit grayer than I remembered, but with the same cheeky grin.

"Barbara!" He still did the best impression of our mother's voice.

"Don't," I shuddered, then grinned at him as we embraced.

I could feel the ribs through his jacket as we hugged, and was struck at how much weight he seemed to have lost, but he looked sun-tanned and fairly well despite this.

"Come and meet Teddy," I exclaimed, just as the dog ran up to us. He jumped up at Peter, and his large paws now almost touched his chest.

"Down, Teddy! I'm so sorry, Peter, I haven't worked on calming him down yet. We've been settling him in and his social skills have got lost somewhere along the way."

"Oh don't worry, Barby, he's a big dog. Where did he come from?" Peter laughed, patting Teddy's flank as Teddy went wild with excitement at the new visitor.

"He was dumped here and sadly, because he's got some, er, toilet issues, we haven't been able to rehome him. Anyway, enough about that, let's have a cup of tea.

"Come on, Ted, let's walk," I called out to the dog and moved in the direction of my trailer, as Teddy instantly obeyed my command to run alongside me and my beloved brother.

"We have seen each other in months. I think it was Christmas, you know," I chatted away, thrilled to be with Peter. As we caught up, we were interrupted by the buzzing of my walkie talkie.

"Excuse me, I must get this," I apologized, while Peter gestured to take the call.

"What do you motley crew want? I've got my darling brother here and so this had better be worth disturbing me for . . ." I said grumpily.

"It is, Barby, I promise. We've got a lady who couldn't keep her cat . . ." Diane's voice was breaking up.

"You don't need to bother me about a cat," I cut over her, "you can deal with that, surely?"

"No, Barby, you don't understand, the cat has nine kittens, and they're all living in your lounge as the cattery is full— we had nowhere else to put them. So you'd better keep Teddy away from your trailer until we find where to put them."

"Oh gawd, too late for that . . ." I said, sprinting off, leaving a bemused Peter standing in the field. "Teddy's already in there, the dog flap is open in the kitchen . . ."

"Oh hell. Barby, get there fast, he'll eat the lot if you don't . . ."

I didn't bother to end the conversation, I just ran hell-for-leather towards the trailer door, gulping for air as I went.

I pulled open the door. "Teddy!" I shouted, then stopped in my tracks.

Peter had arrived a second later.

"What the . . . ?" I said softly as we were both greeted by a scene like something from a film.

Teddy—that huge great big lump of a warrior breed dog—was lying on the floor quietly while nine tiny black and white mewling kittens crawled all over him.

The mother cat lay in a basket, seemingly unperturbed by the giant natural-born predator within spitting distance, playing with her kittens like a doting mother.

"I've never seen anything like that," Peter said in a low voice, so as not to upset the animals.

"Neither have I . . ." I said, shaking my head in bemusement, and admiration. "It shows you what a colossal softie Teddy is. I named him well, after a teddy bear, and here's the proof."

I got onto my knees and bent down to pick up a kitten.

"Well done, Teddy, what a good boy you really are," I said, so proud of his gentleness.

I kissed the tiny fluffy kitten and placed it back down near its mum. The kittens were only a day or two old, and so I just gently took them all off my puppy, and led him outside away from the creatures in case he accidentally hurt them by mistake.

"We can't have you rolling over and crushing one of them, can we?" I said as I stroked him. Teddy settled down next to me, his head on my lap, gazing up at me and blinking occasionally.

Suddenly, Peter, who had been quite quiet, not at all his normal gregarious self, interrupted the peace. "Barby, I need to tell you something."

"What is it?" I said, tearing my gaze away from my beloved pooch.

When Peter first said the words, I didn't fully take them in.

"Say that again, dear . . ." I said, though my head was already spinning.

"Barby, I have cancer, leukemia in fact, and I'm having treatment. I wanted you to know, in case . . ." he said slowly.

"In case of what?" I said, more sharply than I intended.

"In case I die," he finished, simply.

I looked into his beloved face. He meant what he was saying. I was about to laugh it off but something stopped me. At that point, Teddy gave a long moan, the kind of sound that encapsulates sadness. I don't know why he did it, but I almost felt it had come from me, so true, so clear was the meaning behind it.

"You've got cancer, but I won't let you die," I said eventually.

"I don't think you've got anything to do with that. You can't stop it even if you tried," he said, smiling sweetly at me.

For a moment, it felt like we were back in that Anderson shelter, playing Cowboys and Indians while Mother made high tea of fish paste sandwiches and jam tarts. We would use the shelter as a base whether the bombs were falling or not, and it became a fort, a playhouse, the deck of a ship, a submarine and a fighter plane during our many games.

We weren't children now though, we were two adults, facing the cruel reality of being human, being mortal.

"I'm glad you came to tell me. I don't think I'd have liked

to hear news like that in a letter or phone call," I added, not at all sure what to say.

"You know what, Barby, this place is heaven, it truly is. You've created something very special here," Peter remarked, changing the subject, and making me cast my eyes around.

We both sat for a long while, as the sun started to set, as the birds sang their songs, as the earth turned and the planets revolved, but everything felt different.

"Barby, are you okay?" One of the volunteers was peering at me with concern, and I realized I must have looked as though I was a mad old woman, which wasn't far from how I felt the next day. Peter had left around 8 pm and there had been little else to say except to find out when and where his treatment was, and to insist he updated me on a daily, or at least weekly, basis.

Peter had agreed, and our goodbye hug was a strangely emotional experience. I had to wipe away tears as I waved him off, trying not to let him see my distress. He didn't need my fears on top of his own right now.

"Yes, dear, just a little distracted. I must be tired," I said, giving the young girl an absent smile.

"Okay, Barby, I'm going to check on the kittens that came in yesterday with Diane, do you need anything?"

"No, dear," I replied, shaking my head then gazing off into space again. The girl gave me an odd look then left.

"I think she thinks I've lost my marbles at long last," I said to Teddy sadly, "and perhaps I have."

I had been frittering away the morning, making calls to

local businesses to ask them for their donations. The fair was coming up all too soon, but now my heart just wasn't in it. The news of Peter's illness had struck me like a firm right hook. I felt scared one minute, optimistic about his chances of survival the next, then scared and confused again. It was a whirlwind of emotions.

Teddy could definitely sense that something was up. He had been hovering around me all morning, even refusing to join the other dogs in roaming the land. He was by my feet constantly, and I almost stumbled over him a few times.

"Teddy, my darling, I need to walk this way and if you're sitting by my feet, I can't get there. Oh blast this, I can't be bothered to ring people. Come on, Ted, let's go and pot up some plants for the fair, my head is a mess today."

I gave up on speaking to human beings on the phone, and instead wandered over to the greenhouse, which held my kitchen garden close to the gate. The plant pods I'd ordered had arrived; there were about two hundred and fifty of them to pot up over the next day or so.

"I'd better get on with it," I said to Teddy, who gave me a small bark, then settled down on the floor close by, one eye cocked open to see what I was up to.

The rest of the day I spent in solitude, burying my hands in compost and soil, and preparing the plants for sale in August. By the end of the day I'd done almost the whole lot, and was watering them as Diane walked in.

"You look all hot and bothered," I told her, turning back to my plants.

"I've been helping Ian build part of the new storage area

by the horse paddock I'll have you know," she replied. "Is there anything I can do for you before I go?"

"No, thank you, dear," I said. A fly buzzed against the panes of glass.

"Is anything wrong, Barby?" Diane always knew when I was going through something. That said, I've never been a diplomat; every emotion I ever feel seems to be mirrored on my face.

I sighed, putting down the watering can. "It's Peter, my brother. He's got leukemia."

Diane nodded: "I see. I knew something was up. Do you want to talk about it?" she asked, picking a leaf off a young tomato plant.

"Not really. Peter's going to keep me informed, and I've told him he's not allowed to die, I forbid it," I said more confidently than I felt.

"Oh well, if you've forbidden it, death doesn't stand a chance. Come on, Barby, I've put the kettle on. Let's have a cuppa and put the world to rights."

I shrugged, but followed Diane out. Life at the sanctuary had to go on. We had a summer fair to prepare for. We had animals to care for, feed and nurture. We had vet bills and feed suppliers to pay. Nothing had changed, yet everything had.

Chapter 12

WHAT IS TEDDY SCARED OF?

Even though the news of Peter's illness hit me hard, within days I had convinced myself that Peter would battle the cancer and be fighting fit again. I couldn't imagine him being any other way. After the initial shock of Peter's revelation, I started to refocus on what was happening closer to home, in the form of my straggly haired giant mutt, Teddy.

I was pleased to see that his separation anxiety had vastly improved, helped by Diane and I building up the time he spent apart from me, though my hospital stay had knocked him back a little, which was to be expected. I went to my Tuesday darts matches regularly, and had even started going to Saturday night matches again. I'd given those up when Teddy arrived but as time had gone on, he'd got more and more used to trusting that I'd return. Even so, every time I walked across the field towards my home, Teddy would be trying to batter the door down in his urgency to get out and greet me.

It was his nighttime mess that was really upsetting me.

I'd never had a dog that resisted toilet-training to this extent before, and as I didn't have a clue what his background was, I decided it was time to call in a favor from a friend, Brian, who was also a dog behavior specialist. He was a very firm but gentle man, originally from Ireland, and was a qualified animal behaviorist. He was the most experienced dog handler I knew, and his wisdom and intuition in dealing with problem pets was renowned. He'd helped us out with several rescue dogs before, and if he couldn't crack the code on Teddy, then no one could.

"Hello, Brian, thanks so much for coming. There's no need for me to introduce you to Teddy, I see," I joked, as Teddy bounded up to greet Brian, his tail revolving like a helicopter propeller. He stood up on his hind legs to plant his two front paws on his chest, but Brian quickly subdued him.

"Down, Teddy," he said in a low voice.

Teddy obeyed immediately, and Brian fumbled for a treat from his pocket, which Teddy gulped down in one go. Brian had a natural authority that was as loving as it was stern. He was probably in his mid-sixties but he was extremely fit and healthy-looking, his skin permanently tanned from being outdoors all year round.

"He's still very boisterous then," he said, more as an observation than as a question.

I nodded. "He's a very friendly boy." I was always quick to defend Teddy, my devotion was so fierce.

Brian smiled in response. He knew me too well by now to argue. He often worked with private individuals and their pets, especially on issues that arose during the fostering process, so he was well used to dealing with energetic pups like mine.

I didn't like having to ask for help, and I was rarely completely stumped for answers when it came to a dog. Teddy's issue had flummoxed me, and I didn't like that feeling. I was proud of how easily dog rearing and handling came to me, and so when a creature like Teddy, with issues I couldn't resolve, came along, it made me question my own knowledge and instincts. Despite my self-questioning, I had no problem with calling in someone like Brian, even though my pride felt rather dented. I didn't like admitting I didn't know the answer, but I wanted what was best for Teddy.

"How shall we start, then?" I asked, shading my eyes. Even though it was still early in the day, the July sunshine was hot.

"I'll just watch him for now. I can already see he's a well-socialized dog—he's playing with Bessie and Paddington beautifully."

We both stopped to stare at the creatures. Brian was observing, of course, whereas I could simply enjoy seeing the dogs leap and roll, chasing each other in a large circle, and, now and then, fall into mock battles with growling and playful fighting.

I knew enough about what he would be looking for in Teddy. He would check his temperament, and using reward-based methods, look at retraining aspects that might need tweaking, which he'd actually started already when Teddy overenthusiastically greeted him,

Brian would also be looking at his interaction with my other dogs, and even me as well. I was happy to do whatever I could to help Teddy because I knew he couldn't carry on living inside my space with me for much longer if his overnight soiling continued.

"Let's go for a walk," Brian said. He looked pleased with Teddy so far.

In the wild, dogs communicate with their own language of sounds and actions. It is essential for survival that the pack members can send messages and information between each other.

Domesticated dogs can struggle, as they have to adapt to surroundings that aren't the same as in the wild, and particularly if a dog has been rehomed or fostered several times, like Teddy. The whole process would have seemed confusing, frightening and hard for him to understand. I knew this, and I knew that this confusion could be the lingering cause of his mess. Living with humans, even though Teddy was now part of a pack of dogs in effect, would already be tricky for him to understand.

As we started walking, I could see Teddy running over to follow us. His body was relaxed, his tongue lolling out and his ears were relaxed, showing he was a happy hound at that moment.

"He looks very happy to me," Brian announced, cutting into my thoughts.

"I was just musing on that!" I laughed, "so why doesn't he do his business outside like a normal, happy dog?"

"We'll never know for sure, Barby, but we can try to help him. It'll mean you having to get up overnight and take him

out every few hours, though. Do you think you can do that?"
He asked.

I snorted. "I never blimmin' sleep well with five dogs either on top of me or around me, so it won't make any difference."

Brian nodded. "It's obvious he loves play; he loves being
with your other dogs. There are no problems there at all. Look
now, he's bowing with his tail in the air and his front close to
the ground. That's his invitation to play, showing the other
dogs he's happy and relaxed.

"His appetite is good I take it?" he asked.

"Yes, it's excellent. He eats me out of house and home." I
snorted again. "I've never seen a dog wolf down his dinner
as quickly as that pup."

I looked back to make sure all five were following us but
Hercules appeared to have wandered off and so there were
just the four. Bessie was trotting close behind me while Paddington, Wobbly and Teddy played and tussled. The sight of
them all warmed my heart.

"Let's go via the new kittens in the cattery. We had to move
one of the elderly cats into the VIP area to accommodate a
female and her litter of nine babies recently," I chatted, glad
of the company. I always enjoyed walking around my site. It
was where I felt at home, where I belonged—this was my
landscape. I felt as rooted to this ground as the trees and
plants.

We passed by the cattery, at which point all the dogs made
a few cursory sniffs of the entrance while I shooed them away.

"Stay here, I want to check on some kittens, and even though Teddy has proved himself a gentle boy, I wouldn't put it past any of them to decide that they're lunch.

"I won't be a moment," I added to Brian.

"No problem, we'll just stop and see how Teddy responds to commands."

I walked in, confident that Teddy was in good hands. Diane and Ian were both inside the structure that housed a line of cat pens on either side of a small walkway. Trees and plants dotted the area, and there was a small seating area at the far end right by the cat hospital. It was a pleasant spot, and one many of our visitors chose to sit in.

Cats mewed at me, or rubbed up against the chicken wire that kept them contained inside. Each pen had a couple of large, covered platforms that housed the cat's bedding and food areas, and a small ramp, which led up to them. There was a chair, toys scattered across the floor and a branch or shelf that ran down one end so that they could get up high and look at the birds in the overhanging trees.

"Hello, Barby, have you come to check on the kittens? I thought we'd see you before long," she smiled as I entered. "They're in the larger pen right at the end."

I walked down. Ian was standing by their enclosure with two feeding trays, one with water, and the other with dry kibble.

"You can make yourself useful for once, and open the enclosure," he joked. I enjoyed our banter, and didn't mind at all how cheeky he was to me as I gave just as good back to him.

"I'm not your flippin' servant. If you weren't about to

feed these beauties, I'd give you a right hook for that disrespect," I countered, grinning.

"I'd like to see you try," guffawed Ian. "Come on, grumpy, open up, they're hungry."

We went inside. The sight of baby animals of whatever breed, species or type, always brought a smile to my face. They were all noticeably bigger, even though they'd only been with us for a few days, apart from one little creature that mewed rather pitifully, being the last to crawl over to the food that Ian put down.

"The runt," he said, though neither of us needed an explanation.

"I know how that feels," I said. "I was the runt of the litter when I was a child. Perhaps that's why I love the weaker ones so much. I give them the love I never got," I added, a little despondently.

"That's very deep of you, Barby. I don't think I've ever heard you talk like that before. Everything okay?" Ian immediately stopped the banter and became rather serious.

"Oh nothing, just my brother, well, you know . . ."

Everyone on the site knew that Peter had cancer. News traveled fast around here, and everyone had been very sympathetic, asking if there was anything they could do. There was nothing, of course, except to keep the sanctuary running as normal while I absorbed the news of his illness.

There was a pause in the conversation between us for a moment, before Ian chipped in: "Well, if Peter's got you on his side, then you'll frighten the cancer away anyway." I couldn't help but laugh.

It was a standing joke that I was a terrifying harridan, when in fact, I barely reached five foot tall in my boots, hardly an intimidating sight. My temper was legendary though, and anyone unlucky enough to ignite it, usually though cruelty to an animal, would suffer the consequences of a good old-fashioned ear-lashing, as my mother would say.

Back outside, Brian turned to me. "Teddy has done very well so far. He responds well to commands. He understands to come and sit, but he's not so great at staying." He arched his eyebrows at me, implying I hadn't done my work in training him.

"I don't need him to stay. He can live freely here, and as long as he doesn't scare or maul the other animals, and is a friendly dog, *which he is*, it doesn't bother me about the rest." I shrugged.

"Fair enough. He's a bright dog so there's nothing to worry about on that level."

We continued our walk.

"As I say, everything else about his behavior is fine—wonderful in fact—but I'm just stuck with the toilet-training," I sighed.

"Let's go back to the trailer and see what's he like near the dog flap. Perhaps I'll pick up some clues there," Brian said as we turned round and headed back in a loop of about 400 meters.

"What are you scared of, boy? What made you like this?" I murmured to Teddy as he caught up with us. He ran over for a stroke and a quick cuddle before bounding off again.

"Do you think he might have been hurt in a dog flap in

his previous life? Did he suffer some trauma when he was doing his business outside?" I asked.

"I can't answer that, Barby. Let's get him inside and see what happens."

We walked up to the trailer and all four of the dogs that had been following us ran up the steps, Teddy included.

"Nothing I've tried has worked. Every day is the same: I wake up to find he has done his business inside. I know that it's something psychological, just what?" I said, kneeling down in front of Teddy.

"Take him through it and I'll watch you both," Brian suggested, sitting down by the dog flap.

With a soft voice, I said: "Here darling, let's go outside together, see what I've put out here for you, your favorite treat . . ."

I went through the large opening on my hands and knees, which was pretty awkward as there were only two small metal steps outside leading down to the grass.

Again, Teddy pushed past me and went through to find the food without any problem.

"And he can see the other dogs going out at night when they need to go?" Brian asked.

"Yes," I replied, "and I take him out several times during the day, and use the same command to 'do your business' just like I do with the others, and he often does a wee, so he understands the concept . . ."

"During the day . . ." he echoed back to me. He looked up at me, his eyebrows raised. "You don't think he's scared of the dark, do you?"

I paused as the idea sunk in. Why hadn't I thought of that? Everything started to fall into place. He was happy to use the dog flap—during the day. He saw the other dogs doing their business and had even done it himself—during the day. Could all the problems stem from it being nighttime?

"My gosh, I think you've cracked it. I can't believe I didn't think of it myself!" I exclaimed, throwing my hands up. I felt a rush of relief that we might finally have found a solution to the problem that had been plaguing me for months.

"The only way is to test the theory is by trying to take him outside at night. Open the door completely, not just the flap, and see how he reacts. Call me tomorrow and let me know," Brian said, reaching for the door. "I have to go, but I think we may have found the problem, and if I'm right, you have a good chance of finding a solution. Good luck!"

"Thank you, Brian, I'll ring you first thing," I called after him.

"Oh Teddy, are you frightened of the dark?" I said, kneeling down to him. Teddy made that contented harrumphing sound and flopped onto the floor, exposing his belly with his legs in the air, waiting for me to scratch it.

Several hours later, darkness finally fell. I waited up until it was pitch black, at approximately 11 pm, and, yawning, I put the other dogs into my bedroom and shut the door.

"Come on, Ted, let's go outside," I said as I opened the trailer door. This time I was watching his reaction closely. As the door revealed the pitch black outside, I saw what I'd been missing. It was an immediate flinching, a split-second recoil that showed me in an instant that he was frightened.

I shut the door, and Teddy seemed to relax again. He came over to me, his ears flat back on his head still, looking at me almost with reproach.

"You're terrified, aren't you? All this time we've been literally barking up the wrong tree. You wouldn't go out because you've been experiencing night terrors! That's what it is— you're terrified of the dark!"

It all made sense. His reluctance, his repeated soiling, were all because he was too scared to go outside at night. Out here in the countryside, nights were as black as coal. There were few dwellings on our lane, and each was far enough apart to restrict the light pollution to a minimum. We were surrounded on all sides by more land, so of course, there were few other sources of electric light. Each evening I would put lights on well before it got dark because of my eyesight so I could read or watch television. Teddy hadn't showed me he was scared until he really was left to go into the darkness by himself.

"Did something happen to you in the dark, boy?" I murmured, while Teddy sighed with happiness as I stroked his belly. I felt relieved, but deep down I knew I would never truly know the answer.

Chapter 13

THE SUMMER FAIR

"Chris, I need you to come up to the sanctuary today." I was speaking over the phone to our handyman.

"Why's that, Barby? I'm not due to finish the new rabbit hutches till next week," He replied.

"I need you to create a light for Teddy!" I giggled, knowing this would intrigue him.

"Create light? Barby, have you been drinking?" Chris laughed.

"You know I only ever have half a shandy when I'm playing darts," I huffed.

Chris was a kind soul who did lots of work around my land: fixing fences, helping to secure the outhouses for the cat hospital as well as many other smaller jobs. Very often he worked for free, even though he earned his living as a carpenter.

"We literally had a lightbulb moment and discovered what's been the matter with Teddy and his overnight problem," I continued.

At the sound of his name, Teddy appeared—he was never far away from me these days—and placed his head on my lap for a stroke as I told Chris about Brian's guess that Teddy was afraid of the dark.

"Seriously, we think we've cracked it, but to prove it we need to put a good light outside the dog flap so he won't be scared to go out. Can you do that today?"

Chris didn't hesitate. "Of course, anything for you, Barby. I'll come up straight away. You're lucky, one of my regular jobs has just finished so I'm all yours."

"Thank you, dear," I said, really meaning it.

Every now and then, I would be struck by a real sense of gratitude that so many people were willing to support the work we did at the sanctuary, and this was one of those moments. I felt so blessed that time and time again people demonstrated they cared about the sanctuary and the animals contained within our border fences.

We knew that people could be cruel—the evidence was presented to me practically on a daily basis, but this was offset by the kindness, courage and love of my crew and staff members, as well as all the local people who supported us and the many acts of care that took place here every single day.

"I'll drop by a hardware shop before I get to you and pick out an exterior light fitting and bulb. I shouldn't be more than an hour. Bye, Barby."

I put the phone down. Chris was one of the sanctuary's heroes but I knew that if I told him that, he'd be thoroughly embarrassed.

Chris arrived half an hour later, his white van appearing at the gate. I ran over, Teddy at my heels, and let him in.

"Out of the way, you silly dog," I said. "Move over and let Chris drive in."

Teddy had grown so big he reached up to my waist now. He was full of life, a happy, healthy dog in every respect, though still as clumsy as ever.

Our handyman got out, toolkit in hand, and the three of us walked back over to the trailer.

While I made him a cup of tea, Teddy sniffed around him. I heard Chris talking to Ted as the kettle boiled.

"This is all for your benefit, Teddy," he chatted as he worked. "We're putting a light in so you're not scared to go out anymore. Aren't you lucky to have such a caring mummy, eh?

"Is this where you want it?" Chris gestured upward. He was standing on a small stepladder I kept in my extension, and held a light fitting over the doorway.

"Yes, that's perfect. It needs to be as bright as possible for Teddy." I said, peering up at him, Teddy by my side.

"Okay, Barby, I just hope this works."

"Well, if it doesn't then I don't know what I'm going to do with him. I can't cope with him messing inside anymore. This is Teddy's last chance. If he still won't go out then I'll have to take him to the pigsties to stay overnight, and that'll break my heart."

"And his, no doubt," Chris remarked sagely.

I nodded, not wanting to think about the possibility of failure. It had to work, so it was going to.

It didn't take long for Chris to fit the light. When I switched it on for the first time, I squealed with delight.

"This is going to change everything, Teddy, you'll see."

Teddy looked up at me, his twinkly eyes blinking. He gave a short bark, wagged his tail and waited to be stroked, so I duly obliged.

In a few short months, this dog had become my world. I wanted desperately for him to leap this final hurdle, and I couldn't bear to think what I would do if it failed. This was truly Teddy's last chance.

Later that evening, I let all of the five dogs settle in my bedroom, and leaving the door open, I put the usual swathe of newspaper down on the floor by the dog flap. Even though I felt hopeful that we might finally have found the solution, I didn't yet trust it completely.

I made a point of switching the exterior light on and opened the door to show Teddy the floodlit area outside the trailer. Once the door was shut again, I opened the dog flap to show him it was still light out there. Teddy sniffed round the entrance, poked his head out and wagged his tail.

"That must mean something. I know you're an intelligent dog. It's make-or-break time tonight, Teddy." I was speaking to him as if he could understand my every word.

"I want you to go outside here to do your business." As I spoke, I gestured outside, poking my arm through the dog flap and pointing outside.

"That is where you go, just like Bessie, Paddington, Hercules and Wobbly. You go outside. Do you understand me, you great lump?"

Teddy licked my face, forcing me to wipe my cheek and sigh.

"I'll take that as a yes! Let's go to bed, come on, boy."

I slept deeply that night, not waking until the silly cockerels strutted outside my paddock, calling in the dawn at 6 am. I yawned and stretched, then remembered with a start that today was Teddy's day of reckoning. "Get off, you lazy beasts . . ." I muttered as I bolted out of bed, casting off the mound of canine legs, heads and tails that had been all over me.

I headed for the dog flap. It was my sense of smell that gave me the information I'd craved. The newspaper was clean. No soiling, no mess, just a few pristine sheets of yesterday's rag.

I could've wept with delight.

"Teddy, you did it! You did it!" I beamed.

Teddy, of course, was already beside me, giving his tail an exploratory wag.

I clapped my hands and did a small jig around the kitchen.

"You beautiful boy, we found the solution, you're a proper doggie now."

As I skipped, Teddy joined me, barking at the sight of my pleasure and calling the other dogs to witness their batty old owner dancing for joy.

I picked up the walkie talkie. It was past 6 am so I knew Diane would be working already.

I pressed the button and spoke. "Di, are you there? Di?"

A second later, her reply crackled through the speaker. "Yes, Barby. All okay?"

"Come and see this, you have to come," I said, trying to calm myself down.

Teddy was jumping up at me, and as he did so, he knocked a pile of saucepans which lay on the side of the sink and they came crashing to the floor.

"What's going on over there?" Diane laughed.

"Don't worry, just come as quickly as you can," I giggled.

Diane must have thought I'd finally lost the plot.

A minute or two later, Diane appeared and was greeted enthusiastically by the hounds.

"What is it, Barby?" she asked, shaking her head, bemused.

"Look . . ." I commanded, pointing at the floor.

"I can't see anything, just a load of newspaper," Diane replied, looking puzzled.

I looked back at her and watched as the truth dawned on her.

"The paper is clean, which must mean that Teddy went outside overnight. The light worked!" she exclaimed.

"It worked!" I said. "It's a miracle!"

"Well, I don't know about that, but it looks like Brian and you have cracked it at last. But what we don't know is why Teddy was so terrified of the dark in the first place."

That thought sobered me up.

"No, we don't, and we never will, bless him. If only he could tell us." Thinking of what this poor, sweet creature had experienced before he came to live with us broke my heart.

"I'm sorry, I didn't mean to burst your bubble, Barby," Diane apologized, seeing my face. "Let's start again, shall we? It's fantastic news, and it means Teddy can stay living with you."

"You're right, and yes, it does." I beamed again. "Whatever happened is now in the past. Teddy's going to have a wonderful life, and it looks like we've conquered his fears."

"I must get on, I've got a couple coming in at 9 am to look at rehoming two of the kittens, and I've got to do my rounds and get the poorly cats sorted before they come," Diane announced, reaching down to scratch behind Teddy's ears before setting off.

"Alright, see you later. Good luck with the kittens."

We always rehomed siblings in pairs at least, and never let kittens who had grown up surrounded by each other be separated and given away. I hated the thought of them suddenly being forced into solitude in a family home. We were one of the few sanctuaries to insist on this, and I wouldn't back down. If a cat came in to us on its own, then it was rehomed that way. If a litter came in, then, personally, I felt it was cruel to separate them, as I knew from experience that they would often spend days calling for their brothers and sisters in their new home, not understanding where they had gone. It was undoubtedly harder to rehome cats in pairs, but it was in the cat's best interest, so that was my policy and we stuck to it.

Teddy licked my hand to remind me he was there, and I bent down, a great smile on my face.

"Oh Teddy, we got there at last, you brave boy! Well done for going outside. You look very pleased with yourself, and rightly so."

"Now I've got work to do. The fair is fast approaching and I have some final errands to run. We'll go out in the car together later, and collect some of the prizes."

Teddy fixed his adorable face on me, and I reached down to hold it, stroking his ears and tickling him under the chin. What a victory.

The day of the Summer Fair dawned bright and sunny. There were a few white fluffy clouds in the sky so there would be some shade, which was good. We had a lot of elderly people who came to enjoy our special place, and I always worried about them, putting a lot of effort into making sure there were enough chairs and tables, and enough shaded areas to make their time with us as enjoyable and stress-free as possible.

Ian and Arthur had come in early to make sure all the animal fencing was secure, and all the creatures were clean, fed and watered before our visitors arrived.

There were a whole host of young volunteers who were busy on the site too, creating the stalls out of hay bales covered with tablecloths, arranging prizes, displaying gifts, plants and putting out knick-knacks to sell.

A shop had been built a year or two earlier near the entrance. It was a small, low wooden structure with glass walls, but had immediately been requisitioned to keep the cats in. It was the building we referred to as the cattery, along with the other building that housed the area for sick cats.

Already, a young girl with red hair and glasses was arranging homemade flapjacks and tea cakes on one of the hay bales, and setting up a hot water urn to sell cups of tea and coffee. She was writing in chalk on a small blackboard. VEGAN FOOD, it said proudly.

I wasn't a vegan, but most of my staff and helpers seemed to be, and I understood why. It was a choice that I respected, though I liked my Sunday roast too much to give up meat completely.

By 11 am, an hour before the gates were due to open, there was already a queue of people standing outside the Barby Keel Animal Sanctuary. I waved to a few regulars, who were jokingly gesturing for me to open the gates. I laughed and shook my head, knowing that knew I wouldn't budge from the proper opening time of midday to ensure my staff had the time they needed to get ready.

Through the spring I'd potted up hundreds of houseplants, zucchini, and tomato plants to sell, and Diane was busy arranging those. I stood for a moment, watching everyone at work: Ian sauntering past with a wheelbarrow filled with sacks of feed, Arthur going in the opposite direction to shut the workshop where the big machinery such as the tractor, wood-cutting equipment and blades of all descriptions were kept, while Diane looked rather flustered as she rushed around getting everything done before our guests were let in.

"Just got to check on Tiddles," she called as she walked past me, the plant stall ready for visitors to browse.

Tiddles was an elderly cat that she was worried about. He was having problems with his eye, which we were concerned might actually be cancerous, and had various skin problems, which were possibly linked to that. He was clearly suffering, and it had caused Diane a few sleepless nights. She hated thinking he might be in pain, and we were hoping that Stephen might pay a visit today, and if so, even though it was a Sunday, he might treat Tiddles as an emergency and look him over. Otherwise we'd have to wait till Monday, which wasn't the end of the world, but I knew Diane would be fretting.

Midday soon arrived. This was the most important fundraising day of the year for us, raising half of the site's income for the whole year.

I had been distracted from thoughts of my brother and his illness by Teddy, and my relief at finally finding a solution to his issue, as well as the huge volume of work required to get the fair up and running. When I saw a familiar face in the crowd, though, I couldn't deny Peter's illness any longer. It was him. He'd made the effort to come, but my goodness, what a difference a few weeks had made.

He looked gaunt. His skin was gray, his hair thinning. He must've lost fifteen or twenty pounds, and I inhaled sharply in shock at the sight of him.

Peter smiled ruefully as he walked slowly over to me. I gaped, then remembered myself and pulled myself together, hurrying towards him.

"Let me help you, come and sit down, there are plenty of seats," I gabbled. I knew my shock was showing, and the more I knew that, the more awkward I became.

"Don't fuss, Barby, I'm fine, honestly I am," Peter smiled. I could see the outline of his skull through his papery skin. I scanned his eyes, searching for reassurance, trying to find some glimmer of my brother's former good health and vitality.

"It's still me, Barby, come on now, take that worried look off your face. Let's both enjoy the day, I've been looking forward to coming all week." He linked his arm through mine, and I was struck by how frail his arm was. He felt like a stick insect; bony and strange. I swallowed.

"Of course, Peter, though it's customary to tell your sister in advance if you're planning to pay her a visit. I could've set up a special area for you . . ." To my horror, I found I couldn't carry on. There was a big lump in my throat that made the words hard to force out.

"No fuss, please, Barby," Peter pleaded. He squeezed my arm. "It's all going to be fine. Now, I hear you do some delicious cakes here, and I'd very much like to try one."

That was so typical of my brother. He was the one with cancer, yet somehow he was the one reassuring me. Suddenly I felt ashamed of my reaction, as uncontrollable as it was.

"Well then, you've come to the right place. I shall lead you into temptation, also known as our hay bale tea room, decorated by our lovely volunteers, who have been up half the night baking."

I barely noticed the other guests at our fair. Lots of people came up to say hello, or give donations, but my heart wasn't in it. Seeing Peter so fragile had shocked me to my core, and I felt like my head was spinning. Peter had been a fit, tanned and healthy man in his prime. I didn't understand how he could be reduced to this in the space of a few months.

The day passed in a blur. In truth, I couldn't wait for it to be over. Peter, who had taken a taxi from Eastbourne, was driven home by a volunteer after a couple of hours, looking pale and tired-looking. I had insisted we take him back, though I had to stay at the open day as the hostess. I waved to them as they left, but seeing Peter shut his eyes and lean back against the headrest frightened me more than I could say.

When at last the day was over and the last visitor had left, I thanked all my volunteers for all their brilliant hard work, and waved them off, trying my best to keep up a brave face. When at last I was alone, I decided I couldn't face going straight back to my home. Instead, I whistled to Teddy, who had been lying under the shade of a beech tree in the far field, and he ran over, his tongue lolling out as usual, making me smile.

"Let's walk, Teddy. I can't sit still tonight, I've got too much on my mind."

So we walked, and I talked, and Teddy trotted beside me, stopping now and then to sniff at a tree stump, or acknowledge a passing chicken with a small gruff or whine.

My emotions were in freefall. I hadn't really taken the seriousness of Peter's condition on board, believing that doctors were miracle workers, and that anyone with enough spirit could fight off such an illness.

I was hopelessly wrong. Peter had proved that. His condition had deteriorated more than I could've thought possible, and suddenly he looked frail and mortal. How could it be that my brother, who was two years older than me, could look so weak, so helpless in the face of his cancer?

"He was my rock, my golden brother who I adored, Teddy. None of it makes sense. It wasn't so long ago that he was tricking me into eating cow pats, calling them chocolate pies, or telling me to jump into a stream and finding it was barely shallow enough to cover my wet feet. How could that cheeky, naughty, beloved boy be having to face this terrible disease?"

Teddy walked beside me, his quiet presence providing some small comfort through my anguish.

There were no answers, at least none I'd ever understand. That evening, instead of feeling the happiness that a successful fair usually brought, I could only wallow in my fears for the man who had been the light of my childhood.

Chapter 14

BAD NEWS

"**B**arby, can I have a word?" Arthur had popped his head around the doorframe, and he wiped sweat from his brow, almost knocking off his glasses.

"Of course, what can I do you for?" I replied.

"We've had a call from a member of the public saying a horse has been left in some fields over near Eastbourne and it hasn't been fed for months."

"How on earth is it still alive, in that case?" I asked, instantly curious.

"This woman who rang has been feeding it periodically, but according to her, it's simply been left abandoned in the field, no sign of an owner anywhere. What should we do?" Arthur frowned.

I could see this was a tricky situation. The animal would be owned by *someone*, perhaps a farmer or landowner in the area, which meant they were subject to DEFRA, or the Department for Environment, Food and Rural Affairs, which regulated animal welfare and land management.

"We can't just walk up and take the horse, if that's what you're suggesting," I said slowly.

Arthur shrugged. "The person who called has been feeding the horse for months. It's a brown bay and it's literally been left to starve. It would be dead without her, so I can't see there's a problem with taking it—it's obviously unwanted. We can't just sit back and do nothing."

I saw his point, and agreed completely, but unfortunately, we couldn't just take it, it would be theft. There were proper rules and regulations regarding the movement of large animals in this country.

"I agree that poor creature is being treated inhumanely; it's abhorrent that someone could leave a horse in a field to starve. It's disgusting, but there are procedures that we have to follow. However clear it is that the owner is acting badly doesn't mean that we can as well."

It was the end of August, and I was still reeling from Peter's visit three weeks ago. The first signs of autumn were already making themselves present. The evenings were becoming longer and chillier, and I was having to put on a fleece when I did the evening rounds, checking in on the animals before night fell.

"I know, I know. I just get so angry when I hear how cruel people can be." Arthur smiled sadly, and moved into my kitchen, plonking himself down on a spare chair.

"I'll put the kettle on, stay there and we'll work out what to do," I told him, flicking the switch and hearing the welcome sound of the water heating up.

"So, tell me about this woman who rang in. Is she local?"

I asked. I could see that Arthur had got the bit between his teeth over this issue, so I knew he wouldn't let it lie. I also couldn't stand to think of an animal being left to starve to death. In fact, I couldn't imagine of a crueller way to treat a creature.

"She rang in last night. She lives in a cottage that backs onto the field where the horse has been abandoned. It's not an old horse, it's a mare with no obvious signs of injury or illness. It seems that the owner of the land has simply left her. The woman noticed several months ago that the horse wasn't being attended to at all, and was just left in its field. She started bringing apples over, and was surprised to see how thin it was getting, so she started feeding her properly.

"The woman doesn't know who owns the land, but that's something we can try and find out." Arthur accepted the cup of hot tea I'd passed him with a "thank you," before falling silent again.

"Well, in that case, that's where we start. We'll get you and Ian onto it, ask around, go to the council, do whatever it takes to find the owner, then the next step is to approach them. If they don't want the horse, they might be grateful for us taking ownership. It's obvious they're not bothered about it from what the woman says, so it could be resolved quite easily.

"We'll then have to do the paperwork for DEFRA and get her moved here. At least then she can have a good life in our paddock, but don't expect me to come and help move her. Horses are the only animals I'm frightened of. You and Ian can do that, and I'll sort the papers.

"Don't worry, Arthur, I promise we'll get her somehow,

but we have to do it legally," I warned him sternly, and all of a sudden he burst out laughing.

"Oh Barby, I can always rely on you to cheer me up, even if you don't intend to," he snorted.

"What do you mean by that, cheeky git!" I said, rudely.

He laughed, and we continued to tease each other. I relished these moments of downtime with my wonderful motley crew of volunteers.

"How's Peter?" Arthur asked, once we'd stopped insulting each other.

I sighed. "It doesn't look good. When I saw him at the Summer Fair, I just couldn't believe how quickly he'd gone downhill. I hope it's just a temporary setback, but you can never tell with cancer. . . ." We both sipped our tea, lost in our own separate thoughts. I was calling Peter every day to ask how he was, and every day he told me to stop worrying: "Barby, I'm fine, honestly. Since when were you a worrier, eh?" He'd laugh, but often he seemed quite out of breath and that was a new symptom as well.

He always fobbed me off with platitudes, "It's all fine," or "Don't you worry," but despite what he said, I was still worried, and I knew I couldn't conceal it from him.

"Peter, you've just told me you're having chemotherapy so I know this isn't some small thing. Leukemia is serious. People die from this disease, and so of course I'm going to be worried about you."

I'd done some research. I knew that there was only a fifty percent chance Peter would survive for another five years, even with the chemotherapy treatment. These weren't great odds, though it was still something to fight for.

"Do you need any help? The chemo is pretty tough, a good friend of mine had it and, without scaring you, she was very ill with it." I felt like I was begging my brother to let me help him.

He was a proud man, though. "No, Barby, you have enough on your plate running the sanctuary. I've got help. Pam is looking after me between doses of chemotherapy. I really am in very good hands, and I don't want you worrying. I'm going to get through this." Peter was adamant.

I sighed I seemed to be doing a lot of sighing recently. Despite his insistence, I was relieved to hear that he was letting Pam, our younger sister, take care of him.

Before learning of my brother's condition, I hadn't really had a clue about the illness. I'd discovered that leukemia was caused by the bone marrow producing abnormal white blood cells. The abnormal, or cancer cells, grow and stop healthy blood cells from growing by crowding them out in the blood. What I didn't understand was why Peter had got it at all. He didn't have any of the risk factors, such as a history of smoking or HIV, so it seemed that it was just bad luck for him.

We'd spoken only the night before. Teddy was sprawled over me, snoring and twitching, and the other dogs arranged themselves on the sofa and rug while I was on the telephone.

"How's Teddy, anyway? I'd much rather talk about him than bloody cancer!"

I couldn't argue with that.

"Teddy is super. Did I tell you that we've finally fixed his problem soiling? Well, he's just like the others now, he lets himself out at night and does his business outside. It's been marvelous because I can keep him here with me. We're inseparable. Honestly, the thought of him having to move to the kennels was almost breaking my heart."

As I spoke his name, Teddy opened one eye, grunted, then fell back to sleep. I stroked him gently as he dozed, his thick wiry fur feeling rough on my palm.

"I'm so glad to hear that, Barby, that's brilliant news. But I'd better go now. I've got to be at the hospital tomorrow for more chemo," Peter said, yawning at the other end of the phone line.

"Alright, dearest, call me tomorrow and tell me how you get on. I'll be thinking of you," I said, a lump forming in my throat.

"You old ratbag, you'll be too busy to think of me. In fact, I hope you are! You take care and I'll call tomorrow." Peter rang off, and once again, I found myself feeling rather helpless in the face of his condition.

The next day was busy—there were some days at the sanctuary where it felt as though there just weren't enough hours in the day. At 7 pm Ian knocked on the trailer door. I was only just back from helping Arthur clean out the pig pens. They needed very little doing, generally. Pigs were clean creatures and never soiled the place where they slept, so we would usually only have to drag out the soiled hay at the side of their pens, lump a great big load of new straw onto the earth and they'd set about moving it to make their sleep area and their soiling area. Arthur and I stood and watched them at work after we'd finished. The day was still warm by the time they'd finished, and I walked back, Teddy trotting beside me, listening to the evening birdsong and seeing the trees in full green bloom. I made a mental note of how mild, how sweet the air was. The memory of it would have to carry me through the rather long winter days and nights, where I'd crack the ice in the horse troughs at 6 am, swathed in scarves, gloves and thick fleece layers, or tip out the goat pellets with shivering hands. I took a long slow breath in, relishing the space, freedom and simplicity of my life.

"You free, Barby?" Ian asked. "I've got some news."

He didn't wait for me to answer but marched in and sat himself down.

"Cup of tea, dear?" I said, gesturing to the recently boiled kettle.

He shook his head, clearly eager to get down to business.

"I've found the owner of the abandoned horse. It's a farmer out near Uckfield of all places. I was lucky because I got chatting with some friends, and through some farming contacts of theirs, we found the man who owns the land."

Ian explained that the owner had actually been quite pleased to hear from Ian. He was selling his land and therefore no longer wanted the horse.

Listening to Ian talk, I had to hide a smile. I knew how much it would have taken for him to bite his tongue and avoid giving the man a piece of his mind about the way he had treated the animal.

"That's brilliant news, dear. All we need now is to sort the paperwork, but I'm happy to do that for you."

Ian grinned. "Thanks, Barby, I'll be collecting the mare. I might take Arthur along too, depending on how wild it is now. She won't have been handled for a while, apart from being fed by that woman who most definitely saved her life."

We both looked thoughtful at that.

"Thank you for sorting that out, and what a good result—Arthur will be pleased. I told him it would be quite simple to sort." I trailed off, yawning. "Right, I think it's time for my bed," I announced, looking at my watch. It was still very early but I was feeling exhausted. I usually felt more tired in the weeks after the Summer Fair because of the sheer amount of work I had to put in to make it a success beforehand. I was doing fourteen-hour days in the run-up, and I was still shattered.

"I'm no spring chicken anymore," I laughed, heaving myself off the chair. "I'm going to bed to read my book and get an early night."

"Cheerio, Barby, I'll be at the kennels as we're expecting a Staffordshire Terrier to come in at any moment. The owners are having to move out of their rented place tomorrow, and the new place won't let them bring their dog. I think they're going to be pretty devastated, and so I'm expecting a bit of drama tonight. If you hear a car, and see a youngish guy with a Staffie, you'll know it's them. There's no need for you to worry, I'll handle it," Ian said as he got up to go.

"Thank you, dear, you're very good at what you do, and

don't ever expect me to tell you that again. I don't want to spoil you." I giggled at the look on Ian's face.

"I wouldn't expect you to, you old dragon." He gave me a cheeky grin, before whistling a tuneless song and disappearing off up to the sties.

"Time for bed, Teddy," I said. He sleepily followed me, and the others followed suit.

It was only as I was drifting off to sleep that I realized Peter hadn't rung.

"It must be a good sign," I said out loud, making Teddy, who was curled up against the length of me, twitch his head up before dropping it down with a great sigh.

I was deep in sleep when I was startled awake by the sound of the phone ringing. Confused, I staggered out of bed, making the dogs peel off me as I moved. It was still dark out as I stumbled over to the phone and picked it up. Who could be calling me at 6 am?

"Barby? Thank goodness you're awake." It was my niece's voice, my dear brother's daughter. But why was she ringing me so early in the morning?

"Val? Why are you calling me now? What's happened?" I asked gruffly, suddenly feeling panicked. I looked over and saw myself reflected in a sliver of the bathroom mirror. I was disheveled in my T-shirt and pyjama bottoms, my hair unbrushed, and my face puffy still with sleep.

"It's Peter, he didn't react well to the chemo yesterday. They've kept him in but he's really poorly and I wanted to let you know, Barby . . ." At this point she paused.

"What is it?" I asked, suddenly feeling very awake.

"It doesn't look good . . ."

I felt my heart swoop down into my stomach.

"I'm on my way." I didn't say another word. I immediately put the phone down and picked up the walkie talkie.

"Diane, are you there?"

A second later, my friend's voice came through, loud and clear.

"Good morning, Barby, yes I'm here. All okay?"

"I need your help today," I said, feeling like I'd had a pure shot of adrenaline pumped into me. My hands were starting to shake as Val's words started to sink in. *Keep going Peter, hang in there until I get there* . . . became the mantra I was repeating over and over in my mind, even as I spoke.

"Peter's very ill. I'm going to the hospital now."

"And you need me to take Teddy for the day. No problem. I'll be over at yours in five minutes." Diane finished my sentence. She knew what I wanted of her before I'd even got the words out, and yet again I felt a rush of gratitude for the volunteers I spent my days with, and how well Diane knew me after all our years together.

"Thank you, dear." I put the walkie talkie down.

"Teddy, I'm sorry but you'll have to stay. Where I'm going is a place that won't allow dogs."

Teddy looked back at me so solemnly, I didn't know whether to laugh or cry, though I was much closer to tears by this point.

"I've got to get some clothes on before Diane gets here." I bustled into my bedroom, past a yawning Hercules. The other dogs had gone outside to stretch their legs and welcome in the day, but Teddy knew something was up. He wasn't just my shadow; he was my solace and support. I only had a few moments to get ready but I was so glad he was there with me. I felt soothed, much like I did as a child when I cuddled up to my first dog Rex. I would bury my face in his honey-colored fur and weep or wail, or bare my teeth depending on what kind of mood I was in, and I would feel better.

I didn't have time to spend crying into Teddy's fur this morning, but just the sense of him being there, watching me, knowing instinctively that something was wrong, felt so similar that it soothed my soul anyway.

A minute or so after I was dressed and ready to go, Diane appeared.

"I hope it'll be okay," was all she said.

"I hope so too," I replied, bleakly.

I gave a last goodbye kiss to Teddy, holding his great big face and letting him lick my cheek. He followed me out but somehow knew to wait at the gate as I closed it behind me, gave him a last look, then headed to my rusty old banger of a car.

As I turned the key in my ignition, I looked in my rear-view mirror to see Teddy sitting, on the other side of the gate, and I knew in my heart he would be there all day, awaiting my return.

Chapter 15

GENTLE GIANT

I was breathless as I arrived at the hospital, my heart in my throat, afraid of what I might be about to face.

I'd driven faster than usual to get here. The journey normally took half an hour in morning traffic, but today it had taken me less than twenty minutes.

I had left Teddy behind partly because he had an unfortunate habit of falling off the front seat every time I braked. He had never learnt to brace himself, and even though he'd never been hurt because I usually drove at a sedate pace, I didn't want to push his luck, or mine. Also, obviously, he wasn't allowed inside the hospital and I also didn't want to leave him in the car as it was summer. It is shocking how many people leave their dogs in parked cars with no water, and how many die as a consequence.

I felt guilty leaving Teddy behind, knowing he'd spend the day waiting for me by the gate, but today, Peter was more important.

I screeched to a halt in the car park. Luckily, it was still early and there were still plenty of spaces. I fumbled for some change, cursing the fact we had to pay for parking at all in order to see our loved ones in hospital, shoved the ticket on my dashboard then ran in, feeling like I'd run a marathon before I got there.

I wasn't normally one of life's worriers, but Val had sounded so strange, so fearful on the phone, that it affected me deeply. My big, strong handsome brother was fragile after all, and that knowledge frightened me more than I could say.

I scanned the map of the wards at the hospital entrance, searching frantically for the one Peter was on. Walking along the clean corridors of this place, I was struggling to keep my composure. I could feel my heart banging against my chest. Was this the end for my brother?

The ward smelled of disinfectant and sweat. Beds lined each side of the small side ward, and most were occupied with people in various stages of treatment. Everywhere I looked there were machines bleeping, lights flashing, drips pumping fluids into the patients, and people lying dozing or staring out of the window.

I spotted Val almost immediately.

"I'm here. How is he?" I said, breathlessly.

Val smiled, though she looked scared too. People always said that my niece was the spitting image of me. Even her expressions were similar. She had dark blond hair and was petite. She was basically a younger version of me.

Before I could reach Peter's bedside, she took my arm and steered me away.

"Barby, come with me a minute."

Before I could answer, or catch a glimpse of Peter, she veered me out into the corridor. I realized we were standing right by the nurses' station, and I knew that wasn't a good sign. Only the most critical patients were kept this close to the nurses.

I think my mouth was working but no sounds were coming out. I was gripped by a sudden, desperate fear. Peter was dying, perhaps this very day.

"Barby, are you okay?" Val noticed I was now in a state of shock.

"Tell me what it is. Is Peter dying?" I whispered, not wanting him to overhear.

Val laughed, though she didn't take the anxious look off her face.

"Oh Barby, no, is that what you thought? I'm so sorry, I didn't mean to alarm you. He's had a bad reaction to the last chemotherapy session and that's why he's in here. He'll be out again in a couple of days." Val smiled at me as she spoke and rubbed my arm where she'd gripped so tightly.

I breathed, perhaps for the first time since I'd entered the ward a few moments ago.

"I thought . . . I thought . . . Oh why didn't you tell me? I was petrified!" I almost laughed out loud with relief.

"He's still very poorly, Barby. His white cell count isn't good, but they're confident he'll respond to the treatment, once he's had some fluids and some more tests."

"I thought he was a goner," I sighed, feeling my heart in my throat, "and you'd called me in to tell me he was going to die."

"Well, he's not out of the woods yet but he's a fighter, just like you are, and so, with love and care, I'm sure he'll get through this blip," Val assured me. "I just wanted to prepare you before seeing him. He looks very unwell, but I also wanted to ask you to keep upbeat, put a big smile on your face and tell him everything will be fine."

My mind was racing as I took it all in.

"But I thought you said it would all be okay," I said. "Are you asking me to lie to him? I don't mind if you are as it's better we're all as positive as possible, but I want to know the truth." I stared at my niece, searching her face for any sign of concealment.

Val shook her head. "I know you prefer the truth, Barby, it really is just best to present a confident, happy front to Dad. I want him to know that we're all behind him and we'll get through this together."

I nodded. "I understand."

"Let's go and say hello then," she said, putting her arm through mine.

We walked together to Peter's bedside. She had been right to warn me. My brother, Val's father, looked like a skeleton: thin and gray as ash, and weaker than I'd ever seen him. The hospital gown he was wearing seemed to hang off him even as he lay down. I put on my best smile, and with a hearty voice said: "Well then, Peter, what's all this fuss you're making? What on earth have you done to yourself?"

I hoped I was hiding the shock I felt at the sight of him.

Peter opened his eyes and smiled weakly before sinking back onto his pillows. His voice was rasping as he spoke:

"Barby, it's you. It's good to see you. Sorry for all the drama, I'll be right as rain in a few days."

"You can bet your life you will be," I said stoutly. "There's no need to go to these lengths to see me."

Peter smiled. He turned his face to mine and I saw his eyes had sunk into their sockets, which looked bruised. He was as pale as milk, his skin sallow, his voice low.

"It was the last chemo—it wiped me out," he managed to say before shutting his eyes again.

"I can see that, dear, now don't waste your energy trying to talk to me—save it for getting better. Teddy is missing you," I said, feeling suddenly like I could burst into tears. I wasn't a fifty-six-year-old woman, standing there in that ward, looking at my desperately ill brother; I was six years old again, watching out for him to come home from school, my nose pressed against the bay window of our terraced home, counting the minutes until we spotted him, his school tie askew, his satchel swung jauntily over one shoulder, whistling to himself as he kicked stones along our road. He would be carrying his gas mask in its box as war had just broken out, yet he looked like he didn't have a care in the world.

"Peter, it's Peter, he's back," I'd scream with happiness at the first sight of his familiar saunter.

Peter would see me and smile, knowing I would be waiting for him, his greatest fan, his adoring little sister. He knew he was the sunshine of my world and he could've hated me for it, but apart from a bit of teasing or playing the odd trick on me, he was kind and there was always the love between us, which was strong, the heartbeat of my childhood. I could hardly believe that that joy-filled young boy was the same person as the man who lay in front of me now, swaddled in blankets, a drip pulsing into his arm, his skin stretched tightly over his skull.

I sat next to him and gently held his hand. His eyes flickered open for a second, then he fell asleep.

"It's his medication, it makes him drowsy," Val said by way of an explanation.

I nodded.

"I'll stay as long as you need me," I said as Val sat on Peter's other side, taking hold of his right hand. We sat there for what felt like hours, the bustle of the ward around us, people coming in and out, nurses coming to check his drip, to give him medication, to nod quietly at us as we stayed by his side.

By late afternoon, I knew I couldn't put off the work of the sanctuary any longer.

"I must get back to Teddy and the animals," I said, peeling my hand from Peter's and signaling to my niece that it was time for me to leave.

"Thank you for coming, Barby, I'll call you tomorrow and let you know how he is," she said. "There's no need to come back, he's stable now and being given the best possible care."

"Alright, dearest, but I expect a call every morning and evening, right?" I said sternly.

I understood that Val was in charge of managing the situation. It was better for Peter to have as little fuss as possible, and so, with her agreement to ring, I waved goodbye and left.

Back at the sanctuary, I pulled into the drive that wound

up to my gate. There was Teddy, waiting for me, as expected. When he saw the car he sat up, alert. When I got out of the car, he gave a little whinny then a bark. His whole back end was wagging his tail, and he gave a few more high-pitched squeaking sounds as I walked over. He leapt up as I put my hands to the gate, his whole body stretched up, and I saw that he was growing into a huge giant of a dog.

"My gentle giant, I'm so happy to see you," I grinned, and as I shut the gate behind me, he was leaping up for joy, almost taller than me on his hind legs.

"You great softie. Yes, I'm pleased to see you too, yes, you're a good boy." Teddy was beside himself as he ran round in circles, his tongue lolling out of his mouth, which seemed to be smiling. I ruffled his fur, kissed his face and let myself be adored for those few precious moments as we walked back to the trailer.

"I saw you arrive, how are you? How's Peter?" Diane had walked over to greet us, carrying a pile of blankets.

"These are for the FIV cats," she explained, seeing my curious look. "They're old baby blankets that someone donated, which is brilliant. But anyway, enough of that, how's Peter?" She and Teddy matched my stride as we headed for my trailer.

"It's not good news, but it isn't the worst," I sighed. "He reacted badly to his latest chemotherapy, but they've stabilized him and they expect him to recover. I don't know what it means for treating the leukemia but Val will keep me posted."

"It looks like you need a cup of tea," said Di, pulling open the door and ushering me inside.

I felt exhausted all of a sudden. I hadn't done anything physical that day, but the emotional strain was now taking its toll.

"Thank you, dear, that's exactly what I need. Four sugars please," I said, sinking into a chair.

"Tsk, Barby, you know I'm going to keep nagging you about those sugars," she joked, stirring them into my tea when it was poured at last.

We sat sipping our drinks in silence, Teddy curled up by my feet.

I didn't want to talk. I was too tired, and I was feeling rather tearful again, something I didn't want to share with my friend, even though I knew she'd be sympathetic.

"I might just settle down with Teddy and have a bit of peace for the rest of the day. The others can sort everything out, I'm sorry but I'm not up to it," I sighed, guilt washing over me at the thought of letting my crew down.

"Well, thank goodness for that. You've finally learned to delegate!" Diane exclaimed. "I thought it would never happen!"

"Yes, yes," I replied, gruffly. "Tease me if you like. Someone needs to keep an eye on you lot, you know."

I was joking, of course. I trusted my team completely; I was just born to be one of those people who hated asking for help, and probably did too much as a result.

"I'll leave you, but I do have some good news that might cheer you up a bit," Diane grinned at me proudly. "We've just found out that this year's Summer Fair raised almost double what we raised last year." I couldn't help but smile back at her.

"That's brilliant news. Well, that's something positive, isn't it, Teddy?" I cooed, looking into my gorgeous mutt's dark brown eyes.

Teddy rested his head on my lap. He had calmed down from his exuberant greeting, though each time I spoke, he wagged his tail excitedly and nudged my hand with his nose for a stroke.

When Diane had left to carry on with her work, I sat with my dog. The other hounds were out and about as per usual, but, of course, Teddy was with me, my faithful, loving pup.

I knew he could sense that I was suffering. His eyes looked almost mournful as I stroked his tatty ears, and told him about my day.

I confided everything to him. I knew he would keep my secrets and so I told him everything I'd felt that day. I told him how frightened I'd been, how awful it was to see my beloved brother looking so frail, so unlike his golden self. I told Teddy I was scared of the future. I told him that I couldn't see how Peter could bounce back, even though Val had insisted he would be fine. Teddy seemed to be listening to every word. I knew that his breeding made him protective, an excellent guard dog, and intelligent, but I could see now that he trusted me completely and was protective of me in a way that went beyond words.

"All this time, I've thought it was me who helped you, but I was wrong wasn't I? It's you who's been helping me all this time. It's you who's saved me," I said softly, putting my face to Teddy's neck and holding him in a little cuddle. Tears were rolling down my face. I didn't care, it was only my dog who saw them, so I let them run and run. Teddy's fur was prickly against my cheeks, he smelled of summer grass and that indescribable doggie smell which I breathed in slowly, letting the emotions of the day flow through me, my trusty companion helping me through each second of my pain.

I had spent many hours with him, teaching him to trust me, making sure he knew I'd always come home to him. I made sure he was fed at the same time each day, had plenty of good long walks to calm his boisterous nature, and I'd cleaned his messes for weeks and months, but it was all repaid a thousand-fold in that moment.

Chapter 16

PETER SICKENS

The mornings were darker now that autumn was setting in, and colder. I would pull on a fleece, long trousers and work boots at the start of each day in order to go out and help my team with the early morning chores.

A thick dew lay across the fields, which were cloaked in a fine mist in the early morning. The beech, ash and oak trees were in various stages of renewal, with glorious shades of red, brown and orange leaves, creating a backdrop of intense beauty.

I shivered as I pulled my clothes on one morning, shortly after I'd visited Peter in hospital. Outside, the cockerels were still crowing intermittently, as though not quite sure whether it was time to wake up.

"They really haven't got the hang of being cocks, have they, Ted? Ted?" I looked around. He wasn't beside me. There was only Hercules, dozing as per usual, and Bessie who was looking at me with reproachful eyes because I hadn't yet got up to make her breakfast.

Just then a clatter of the dog flap being opened, followed by the sound of paws padding across the floor announced the return of Paddington, Wobbly and Teddy.

"Ah, there you are, pesky dogs," I said, affectionately. "Ready for your breakfast, I suppose?"

The day was set to be a busy one. We were due to have a new FIV cat arriving at some point from Romania, but as was often the case, we had no idea what time it might arrive, which meant that someone would need to be on call overnight.

I looked up and burst out laughing. All five dogs were lined up by their bowls, sitting and waiting for me to feed them. When I looked over, each one started wagging its tail, five sets of eyes staring back at me.

"What a funny lot you are. Here you go," I said, reaching for several tins of their favourite dog food and the dry biscuits. "You can start on those," and I deposited a few handfuls of dry kibble into each bowl, which were eaten within seconds.

I spooned out the food, making each dog wait their turn. They stood like sentries in their line, awaiting their main meal, swooping down to feast before the bowls had even touched the floor. I watched them with satisfaction, especially Teddy, who was doing exactly the same as the other dogs.

Eventually they all finished, their bowls licked clean, and I opened the door for them to depart. Teddy stayed by my side, of course, coming over for a cuddle and a stroke before I set about making myself some tea and toast.

I had the same breakfast every day: a single slice of toast, beans and a grilled tomato. I had so many decisions to make each day that I'd long since decided that the basic stuff, such as food, needed to be kept simple so I could focus on my animals.

I was about to head outside when my phone went. I picked it up to see that it was Val. My stomach dropped and I felt a sudden wave of nausea.

"This can't be good news . . ." I muttered to myself as I reached for it.

"Val, is everything okay?" I couldn't keep the emotion out of my voice, and I realized my hands were shaking.

My niece's voice was calm, reassuring even. "Now don't fret, Barby, but Peter's been taken ill again. He's back in Eastbourne Hospital."

Teddy wandered back over to where I was standing, and sat down heavily, resting his head against my knee. Somehow, again, Teddy knew that something was happening, and he was showing his support for me.

"Right, dear, well, what's happened? How long has he been in for? What have the doctors said?" I gushed.

"Slow down, Barby, he's okay but he's poorly," my niece said.

"I don't mean to be rude, dear, but of course he's poorly, he's got leukemia and now you're telling me he's back in hospital."

"I know, I know. Look, I don't want to worry you but I have to be honest. It doesn't look good. Dad has gone downhill since that reaction to the chemo. His body just wasn't strong enough to handle it and he's very poorly indeed."

As Val's words sank in, I felt a sudden desire to weep.

Was this the end for Peter? And if so, what would I do without him?

"Can I come and see him?" I asked, my hand instinctively moving to stroke Teddy's head and ears.

"Of course you can, Barby, though it might be best if you wait until visiting time this afternoon to give the doctors a chance to do what they need to do," Val said. I couldn't shake off the feeling she was trying to soothe me, like a child, and I worried that she perhaps wasn't telling me the whole truth about the gravity of Peter's condition.

"Alright, dear," was all I could say, "I'll see you later."

I put the phone down, pausing for a long while until my head felt clearer. I tried my best to console myself, to hope that it would all be okay, but there was a feeling of dread at the pit of my stomach that I just couldn't shake off.

"Barby, are you there?" Di's voice coming from the walkie talkie interrupted my thoughts.

"Yes, dear, I'm here, sorry, I'm on my way down," I said, trying unsuccessfully to keep the wavering tone out of my voice.

"Everything okay?" Diane asked, and I shook my head though she couldn't see me.

"It's fine, dear, I'll be there in a tick." I looked down at Teddy, though Teddy was fast catching me up in height. He stood at least thirty inches tall now, his shaggy fur making him seem even larger. His tail was between his legs, and he looked like he was waiting for me.

"Come on, Ted, let's go and start our day again. We have

to put Peter out of our minds until later. It's the only way I'm going to be able to concentrate on everything I have to do."

I was glad of Teddy's company that day. He sensed my disquiet, and never left my side.

"Crikey, Barby, that dog really is your shadow," one of the new volunteers remarked, a young man called Terry.

I smiled but I didn't have the heart to banter back. I couldn't focus that day, however hard I tried.

"Barby, what time did you say the FIV cat would come in?" Diane asked as she washed out the cat bowls.

I looked at her blankly, like she'd asked me when I was next going to the moon.

"What on earth is the matter, Barby? There's something wrong, I can tell. You're normally joking or telling someone off or going gaga over one of the new intakes in the kennels. You're not yourself today and Teddy knows it. Look at him sitting over there, waiting for you."

We both looked over to where Teddy was standing outside the cordoned-off FIV area, on the other side of the chicken wire that separated the sick felines from their FIV-free counterparts.

Seeing us both stare back at him, Teddy submitted, lying on the ground and giving a little whine, as if to say, "I'm here, Mummy."

Suddenly there was a shout from the entrance, and the sound of a car horn.

"What's going on out there?" I asked, alarmed.

"You'd better get over there," Diane said, and I nodded my agreement.

Running towards the commotion, Teddy at my heels, I saw a large vehicle with a horse box attached, beeping at the gate. Ian was standing at the back, and it was then I could hear the sound of hooves kicking at the sides of the metal container.

"It must be the starved horse," I shouted as I ran over, opening the gate. By now there were quite a few volunteers on the scene. The vehicle drove in, Arthur at the wheel, and Ian followed. He was grinning but he had a huge bruise on one side of his face, and I gasped at the sight of him.

"I copped it a bit. She's semi-wild now!" he laughed.

"Well, I wouldn't be grinning from ear to ear if a horse had just kicked my face!" I exclaimed.

"It's fine, she'll be alright. We've got her, and that's all that matters," Ian said. "Now we've just got to get her out again, but I think this will be the easy bit."

I followed the vehicle as it drew up next to the main paddock. The men must've moved our usual resident horses into a separate field as there was no sign of them.

Ian opened the rather rusty gate, and Arthur backed up to the entrance, surrounded by at least ten of us onlookers who had dropped everything to watch this spectacle.

Bash, bash, BASH!

Teddy flinched at the sound of the angry horse, whose hooves were pounding at the side of the box. I wouldn't have put myself in Ian's shoes for all the money in the world.

Arthur had stepped out of the parked car and was standing

by at the side of the box. Ian gave him a nod, stepped forward and unlocked the catch at the back, throwing it open as quickly as he could, and keeping behind the door to minimize his risk of further injury.

There was a moment's pause, then, in a clatter of hooves and a flash of brown, the mare tumbled out of the box, shaking her mane angrily, and stampeded off to the far corner of the field.

"Quick, shut the gate!" I yelled, taken over by the unfolding drama.

"Don't worry, Barby, we're on it," Arthur shouted back. Thankfully, Ian had already leapt into action. He shut the gate and climbed up to stand on the metal bars that formed it and look over at the disgruntled, but thankfully now rescued horse.

"She'll be okay. She's had a shock. It took us quite a while to bridle her, which is how I got this," he said, rubbing his cheek. "I'll keep an eye on her today, put some food and hay out, and see whether she'll let me approach her tomorrow. Give her some settling in time."

He was already watching her intently. The horse was perhaps thinner than would be ideal but I was relieved to see she wasn't too sickly-looking.

"She's a beauty though, Ian. I still don't know how you ever managed to restrain her for long enough to get her into the box."

"Practice and lots of it," he winked.

"I must get back," I said, remembering that I had to make myself a quick lunch before heading to the hospital.

The delight I'd felt at seeing the neglected creature run free in the care of our sanctuary instantly vanished at the thought of Peter, leaving behind a sick feeling in my stomach. I couldn't bring myself to finish my sandwich, so I said good-bye to Teddy, who walked me over to the gate again, and waved to Diane that I was off.

Every second of that drive was agony. I didn't know what I was about to face and I had no idea how I was going to feel. I didn't know if Peter would survive this cancer. Everything felt strange and unsettling. I walked in to that ward a little slower than last time. By now I was dreading what I might see.

My instincts weren't wrong. Peter was lying against the starched white sheets, his eyes shut but his forehead creased with pain, numerous drips attached to his arms, and machines around him.

I gasped in spite of myself and I hoped my brother hadn't heard me. I was relieved to see his eyes flicker open as I reached his bedside.

"Peter," I whispered. "Hello, darling. How are you feeling?"

"Pretty rough," he managed to say, though his speech was slow and his voice low.

I nodded. What could I say? Nothing I could do or say would take away this terrible condition from him or make him feel any better.

"We rescued a wild mare today," I said, not knowing why. "She's beautiful but unmanageable. Ian was kicked in the face, he could've been seriously injured, but he loves horses. He loves their wildness."

I knew I was babbling but I really, truly had no idea what to talk about. I wouldn't reassure him because I didn't want to lie. I have always prided myself on my ability to be honest, no matter what the occasion and no matter how hard that can be. I wasn't a hypocrite, and I wouldn't start by telling fibs now. So instead, I told him about the joyous, wild look in the mare's eyes as she galloped off. How her mane tossed against her rich brown body, as brown as the leaves on the trees.

"She just ran for her life once that box was opened. She looked like she would run until she dropped, except there was a fence to stop her. She isn't properly free, I know that, but she's safe now, and she'll be fed every day by Ian, and adored if I know him."

Peter blinked. One of his machines made a regular clicking sound. A nurse appeared, adjusted his bolus, then turned round to leave.

"Please, how is he?" I asked. She smiled sympathetically but said, "I'm sorry, my dear, you'll have to wait for the doctor. They'll be doing their rounds in about an hour."

"Okay, dear, thank you," I said, and turned back to Peter. "I might as well make myself comfortable then, and I can tell you all about the new cat coming in today. He'll have had quite a journey to get to us."

I chatted away quietly, telling Peter everything that was going on. The life of our sanctuary was ever-changing. Animals came in every day, others were rehomed, while the sick and unwanted beasts were given a home for the rest of their days with us. Peter drifted in and out of consciousness as I spoke, but I had a feeling he was enjoying what I was saying.

A small smile played around his mouth, and I held one of his hands. I could have spoken for hours, but eventually, the doctor came.

"How are you feeling, Mr. Keel?" the consultant asked. He was an Asian man with spectacles and a polite manner.

Peter shook his head a little.

"He hasn't really said a word," I interrupted. "How ill is he really?"

The doctor looked at me. "And you are . . . ?"

"I'm Barby Keel, Peter's sister," I replied. "Please tell me what is going on."

"Come this way, Miss Keel," he said, saying a quick goodbye to Peter, as he led me away from the bed.

"As you know, your brother is very sick," he said.

"Is there anything we can do?" I asked, searching his face, hoping he would be unflinching with the truth.

He shrugged. "There is a possible way . . ."

"What is it?" I jumped on his words. I was willing to go to any lengths to help my brother.

"We can test you for a possible stem cell match," he answered.

"What would that mean?" I asked.

"There's a one in four chance you'll have matching bone marrow, which means we can transplant stem cells in order for Peter to undergo more chemotherapy."

"What happens if we don't match?"

"Without a match there's little more we can do for Peter, except to make him as comfortable as possible." A silence seemed to follow those words. Even though I knew we were

standing in a busy ward of a large hospital, the world seemed
to stand still for those seconds while I digested this latest de-
velopment.

"So you're saying that if I match Peter, then he can have
some of my cells, and then he can have more treatment?"

"That's exactly it. That would be a Matched Related Donor
or an MRD transplant. It's a simple blood test, where we'd
look at HLA typing or tissue typing. We'd be looking at the
proteins on the surface of your blood to see if they match
Peter's. The proteins are called HLA markers, and the test
would show us if you're a match with Peter—"

Before he'd finished speaking, I said: "I'll do it, and do
you know what, I reckon everyone at my sanctuary will do it,
and our friends and supporters. We'll all take this test, and
we'll find a match, we have to."

The consultant looked at me gravely. "You heard the odds,
Miss Keel; it's only a one in four chance of a relative being a
match, let alone anyone unrelated. Please don't get your hopes
up. . . ."

I looked back at him. "What else can we do?" I asked,
bleakly.

He shook his head, a look of regret on his face, patted my
arm kindly, then turned to carry on his ward round, leaving
me feeling more hopeless than I could ever have imagined.

Chapter 17

GOODBYE

Many studies have shown that dogs can read human emotions—they can literally pick up on our joy and sadness. Animal behavior experts have proved time and time again that our four-legged friends can pick up on our expressions, through our voices, actions and the way our faces change. Any dog owner already knows that our pets are sensitive to our moods, and can display sympathetic behavior when we are sad, or joyful actions when we're happy.

Our dogs not only read moods by seeing and hearing how we react, but they can smell our feelings, especially if we are fearful. By sniffing us out, dogs can adjust themselves and their moods to model ours, which is why a canine becomes scared and defensive if we react with fear.

If I needed proof of a dog's ability to mirror and reflect back the way I was feeling, I had it now with Teddy. Over the weeks, as Peter's condition deteriorated, as my stress levels increased, as I grew tired and weepy after each hospital visit, Teddy never left my side.

When a dog experiences a stressed or unhappy owner, they tend to seek more reassurance. They stick close to their owner and ask for more strokes or affection than normal. It is the scent of distress they are reacting to, and their instincts are to keep close, to give and receive more love, thus deepening the bond between animal and human.

Teddy could sense my angst. From the moment I opened my eyes to the moment they shut again at the end of the day, my dog was there beside me. Every few minutes he'd nudge me for a tickle or a gentle stroke, which I did absent-mindedly. My heart was in turmoil. My beloved brother was dying, and I could barely think about anything else.

I'd had the blood test suggested by the doctors. It took a second, yet it was the most vital piece of the jigsaw, the test that could mean life or death for my brother.

I had been devastated when the consultant pulled me into the corridor a day later to give me the truth of the results, and Peter's condition. I could tell immediately that it wasn't good news. The consultant looked grave, and I felt my heart skip a beat.

"Tell me," I said.

"I'm sorry, Miss Keel, but you weren't a match, and that means it's very unlikely that anyone else will be."

I paused for a moment.

"What about my sister, Pam, have you tried her?" I asked.

"We have, and I'm sorry, it's the same news . . ."

The doctor looked abashed, his face was sympathetic and I could tell we had been the last resort for finding a solution for Peter.

I stood there for a moment, the ward fading away. I could almost smell the new baby scent of talc and milk, when Mother presented Pam to Peter and me only minutes after giving birth to her in the bedroom of our terraced home. We stood together, thick as thieves, goggling at this new creature in Mum's arms.

"She's lovely," said Peter simply.

"Her face is all screwed up like a pig," I giggled, making Peter nudge me with his elbow, trying to shut me up. He always looked out for me when it came to my mother.

"Trust you to say something so horrid—bad girl, Barbara. Go and wash your mouth out with soap," Mum said, and at that moment Pamela squawked for food, making Mum usher both of us out of the room.

"Why did you say that?" Peter had said as we tumbled out. I shrugged. "Don't know." Peter sighed.

"Come on, Barby, race you to the park."

Standing outside the ward that day, I felt a sense of deep grief and helplessness, knowing that even between us siblings we couldn't save him.

"Is everything okay, Ms. Keel? I know it must be quite a shock."

I nodded. Then I shook my head. I didn't know how to react to the news that there was little hope for my brother.

"What happens now? What happens to him if we can't do a bone marrow transplant?" I asked at last, my voice wavering.

It was the doctor's turn to shake his head. "We can keep trying to shore Peter up, but without a transplant there's very little we can do. We can't repeat the chemotherapy. He's too weak. All we can do now is try to keep your brother as comfortable as possible."

People say that experiencing grief is like standing in a vast ocean, with waves breaking over you. That's how I felt at that moment. I could barely take in the words I was hearing, but deep inside I knew that this was the end for Peter.

"Thank you, doctor," I said at last.

He gave me a small smile, touched my shoulder with his hand, then walked away, probably to another relative of another patient who wouldn't make it through either.

I didn't envy him his job; for all the status and money in the world, I couldn't do what he had to do. Telling someone their loved one was beyond medical help, well, I couldn't think of anything worse.

Val had taken a break, and so I waited until she returned with coffee for herself and a tea for me, before telling her what the consultant had said.

My niece nodded. I looked at her face and there was no shock there, no surprise.

"You've known all along, haven't you?" I asked. When she put her plastic cup down, I gripped her hand. "You knew, didn't you?"

I looked into her lovely blue eyes and she took in a great big breath, sighing it out before replying.

"Oh Barby, yes, I did know. Peter hasn't got long left. He's very poorly. I'm sorry I didn't tell you sooner. I knew about the test result, how could I not? If there had been any chance at all of him surviving, the doctors would've been straight on to you or Pam, or me. . . ."

"You knew?" I stuttered, my head spinning with this revelation.

Val nodded, her eyes brimming with tears. I looked at her face and saw how she'd tried to protect me from the truth, and I couldn't hate her for it; in fact, I loved her more. I would have done the same, if it'd been me in that impossible position.

"It's okay . . . it's okay." I shushed her like a child as she dissolved in sobs.

There were two chairs just outside the ward, and so I steered her to them, and we sat there for what seemed like ages, saying very little, and letting the truth sink in. Peter wouldn't ever be leaving this hospital. He would never go home.

I made my way back home slowly that night, driving the familiar route automatically, without thinking. When I finally reached the gates of the sanctuary, I stopped for a moment, barely able to think about talking to people. I knew I needed to see if the FIV cat had arrived from Romania, though, so I reluctantly dragged myself over to the cattery to see what was going on.

What happened next sums up the spirit of the Barby Keel Animal Sanctuary, the people and animals who cared so deeply about each other.

"I'll have the test," a volunteer called Tina announced,

when I recounted to Diane and the others what had happened at the hospital. Tina had recently divorced her husband and had started volunteering with me to help her get over the shock of her marriage ending. She had blonde hair, expensive-looking jewelry and designer wellies. I didn't care how much money she had, or didn't have. It took all sorts to volunteer here. I had people without two pennies to rub together alongside wealthy people with big cars rolling into my driveway. All I ever cared about was how they treated the animals, and the work they did for us. That's how I judged people, and Tina was no different.

"So will I," said Di.

"And me," said Chris.

They were all sitting on the iron garden chairs outside the cattery, sipping tea and shivering a little with the cold.

Once Tina had put herself forward, then Diane and Chris, everyone else followed suit. Over the next few days, people rang the hospital and went along for tests. I could barely say thank you, I was so moved by their generosity, yet I knew the chances of anyone apart from a relative or family member being a match were almost non-existent.

No match was found, and I had to accept that Peter had just weeks left to live. I don't know how I got through those long days. I went through my chores like a robot, barely eating or sleeping, and hardly noticing what was going on around me. Teddy lay beside me each night, stirring regularly to look up at me, his great body sprawled across the bed, leaving me with a few inches down the side to lie on. I didn't care. I knew

I wouldn't sleep anyway, and each night I lay there, dreading the inevitable news.

The worst thing was the prospect of telling Dad.

He had seen Peter at the Summer Fair a few months ago and saw how frail and thin his son had looked. For a man who hated showing emotion, my dad looked like he was on the verge of breaking down. My role at each fair is to be the hostess, to greet people, chat to those who support us and make sure we put on a happy face; I didn't want my father to feel like he had to do the same and so I'd led him back to the privacy of his trailer and let him rest and try to deal with the shock of Peter's appearance.

So although Dad had known Peter was ill, I'd then done the same thing my niece had, and protected him from the grim reality of the situation. Dad was a fragile, sensitive man, and generally rather a loner, preferring the company of the animals, rather than the humans, at the sanctuary. He dealt with things in his own way and in his own time. When my parents separated, Dad moved into the trailer I bought for him and never said a word about the break-up.

I found it difficult to talk to him about the gravity of Peter's illness, but as I knocked on his trailer door after the volunteers had left, part of me regretted not telling him the truth sooner. How would he react knowing his only son was now dying?

"Dad, I'm sorry, I know this will upset you, but I have to talk to you about Peter. His condition has got worse and it looks like he's fading fast."

Dad looked over at me, blinking as he took in what I was saying.

"Come and sit down," he said, and I knew he was trying to make this easier for me to deal with. That was so like him. He was so thoughtful, so quiet and unassuming. I felt very protective of him, even though he was my father.

"It's not good, and the doctors think he may only have a few days left. Do you want to go and say goodbye? I can take you up there if you want to go."

Dad looked down at his hands, gnarled by hard work and the seasons. He seemed to take an age to make his decision. Eventually, he shook his head.

"I don't think so, dear. Just tell him I'll be in soon and leave it at that."

I understood how Dad felt, although I knew others might find his decision unfathomable. Who wouldn't go and see their child if they were dying? But Dad hated hospitals, he couldn't stand seeing his loved ones suffering, and he would've been broken by the experience of going in. Peter knew all this. Dad seemed to think that by going into hospital, he would alarm Peter, making clear to him that there was no hope left. Somehow in Dad's already grieving brain, he thought he was doing the right thing by not going to the hospital.

"But Dad, he knows he's very ill. He knows there may be little hope left."

Tears were now rolling down Dad's face. I'd never seen him cry before and the sight shocked me profoundly. I tried to convince him to see Peter but he was adamant, and I could see how he was suffering so I didn't push it any further.

"If you change your mind, I'll take you, no matter what time of the day or night . . ." I added, squeezing his rough hand and wiping away the tears that were springing from my eyes too.

I saw that Dad, such a deep-feeling man, would sacrifice his own longing to see Peter in order to save his son from any more suffering. I realized that Dad was trying to protect him from the truth, even though it meant losing the chance to say goodbye.

I swallowed hard at that, feeling my own emotions welling up.

"Okay, Dad," I nodded, "that's okay, I'll be up there tomorrow and I'll say you'll be in just before Christmas . . . He won't last that long," I added, almost as an afterthought.

It was Dad's turn to nod.

We sat in silence, the weather gloomy and cold, staring out of his small window. We had gone beyond words. There was nothing left to say. Peter was dying. Dad knew and somehow we had to keep going, plodding on with life as both of our hearts shattered.

Christmas was fast approaching, and as the temperature dropped and we awoke each morning to the fields coated in a white frost, Peter's condition worsened. I knew that he wouldn't see the New Year, and so I'd asked him what his last wish would be. He knew his time was ending, and I wanted to do everything I could for him.

"Take me home to yours for Christmas Day," he'd whispered.

"You want to come to mine and have a proper Christmas? Of course, Peter, anything for you."

Peter tried to prop himself up to talk, and it broke my heart to see the effort it took just to lift his head.

"Don't force yourself, dear. I can hear you just fine, so you go ahead and tell me what you want," I said, gripping his hand as I leaned in to hear him.

"I want . . . I want to see a proper wood fire before I go . . ."

I nodded, understanding that he wanted that special feeling of comfort and safety that a fire brings in mid-winter. I used to have an open fire in the large prefabricated home I'd built with Les. Peter was confused, as that place was long gone now. The knowledge that he'd recalled our happy evenings there together during the times he'd visited, sitting in front of the fire sipping hot chocolate and reminiscing, brought fresh tears to my eyes that I had to blink away.

I knew the hospital would never let Peter out as he was too poorly, and so I racked my brains to think of a solution.

I was still pondering over it when I got back to the sanctuary that night, and I mentioned it to the volunteers.

"What about your electric fire? It has a proper flame effect on it and so it would at least look like a proper fire," Arthur suggested.

"Of course! Why didn't I think of that? I must be going scatty in my old age," I said, delighted at the solution. "I can take the fire into the hospital and he can have it by his bedside."

Except I wasn't allowed.

The nurses shook their head when I told them my plan the next day. I was visiting every day now, each day not knowing whether it would be the last time I saw Peter. Val and I would take it in turns to sit with him, read the newspaper to him or just sit beside him in case he woke up, so he would know that there was always someone with him.

When I heard the word "no," I felt like erupting in fury, but I managed to contain it. Deep down, I knew that what I was really angry at was the idea that my brother could be lying in a hospital bed dying of cancer while I was fit and well.

"Please let me bring it in," I pleaded, but the nurse just shook her head apologetically.

"I'm sorry, darling, but we can't do that." She was a large Filipino lady who had been very kind to Peter, so I didn't shout or scream, or make a fuss. I knew I had to abide by the hospital rules though I've always hated being told the word "no."

In the end, the decision was taken from us.

That night, I was jolted awake by the sound of the telephone ringing. All five dogs stirred, and I felt my heart in my throat as I picked up the phone.

"Please, God, no . . . please, God . . ."

Val's voice was at the other end.

"It's time, Barby."

I swallowed hard. "I'm on my way."

It was like *Groundhog Day*. I drove back to the hospital. Put money in the meter. Walked the lengths of the shining corridors. Smiled at the nurses at their desk, who waved me to Peter's bedside.

"Thank you for coming." Val was already there, holding onto Peter's left hand, while I sat down at his right side.

"They say it won't be long now," my niece told me, the tears visible in her blue eyes.

I nodded wordlessly.

"Who's looking after Teddy?" she asked.

"Di," I answered, my voice croaky. "Diane will have him. She knows what to do at the sanctuary, we don't need to worry."

"What do we do?" I asked my niece, suddenly uncertain.

She shook her head. "I don't know, Barby. I suppose we just have to wait. What else can we do?"

At the sound of my voice, Peter opened his eyes.

"Hello, you," I said quietly, stroking his hand as gently as I could, "it's your horrid, ratbag of a sister, Barby. You're being such a nuisance," I teased, trying to keep my voice light and knowing that he would appreciate my banter. "You're just grabbing all the attention by being in here. You always were the one who got the attention . . ."

Peter blinked and smiled. He rasped "Hello" but it was clear he was fading fast, and so he fell into silence, staring through the window at the gray skies of the day that was just beginning.

All at once, I was hit by a slew of memories, and I blurted them out, not really knowing if Peter was listening anymore.

"Do you remember my frog, Prince Charming, the one

that lived in the Anderson shelter?" Peter shifted in his bed. His sheets were tangled around him, so I started to tuck them back in properly, and talked as I went. I didn't wait for a reply.

"One night during the bombings, I lost him, and that, to me, was scarier than being hit by one of those German shells. Do you remember Granny Grunt and Grandad Whiskers wrapping us up in blankets when it was cold overnight as we sat inside the shelter, waiting for the bombs to stop. And the sound of the all-clear siren . . . I don't think I'll ever forget that wail, the relief . . .

"And the day we returned home to find our house had been destroyed. It was just a pile of rubble and smoke, and all I was worried about were our toy rabbits!

"Wasn't it kind of the firemen to go in and find them? They could've been hurt. They could've said no, but they went in and got us back our fluffy bunnies. I'll never forget that; it was the kindness that I really remember about the war . . . and the cows! Do you remember the cows and the fields when we were evacuated? I'd never seen anything like them before. I loved the feeling of space, of running through the fields and feeling like we could run together forever. What larks we had as children, what fun, what freedom. And you, you were always the beloved boy, the good boy, the handsome child, whereas I was always the scrawny misfit. Nothing ever changed. Mum always loved you more and I couldn't blame her, Peter, I really couldn't."

At that, I stopped talking. I realized my cheeks were wet with tears; the memories flooding back had broken the dam.

My brother was dying, and there was nothing I could do about it. Nothing at all.

The day passed. Val had rung me on Thursday, the 20th of December, just five days before Christmas. The wards were as cheery as they could be with tinsel and a fake tree at the entrance, but I didn't care about any of that. Christmas meant nothing to me while my brother lay stricken, as we counted his last hours on earth. Val and I stayed through that day, through Friday, and then, at some point overnight between Friday and early Saturday morning, I dozed off in the chair next to his bedside.

The ward was quite dark when my niece shook me awake. At first, I felt disoriented. I didn't know where I was, then I saw Peter's still body lying on that bed, under white sheets, and I knew without being told.

"He's gone, Barby. It was so sudden. I'm so sorry . . ."

It was the early morning of Saturday, the 22nd of December.

I looked back at Val. Her mascara had run down her face with her tears and her face was crumpled.

I held her hand, feeling like part of me had gone with Peter.

"He was your father, I'm sorry too," I said, blinking away the sleep. We stood there next to each other for a few moments. Other patients on the ward were starting to wake up, machines made their soulless bleeping sound, but around Peter there was nothing but silence. Val had called a nurse and she hurried over to check his pulse. Finding nothing, she shook her head sadly at us both, then started the process of untangling my brother from the drips and wires.

I watched, holding Peter's hand for the last time. His face was white as chalk, and it was screwed up as if he'd been in pain, but perhaps that was how people always looked. I couldn't fathom how he could be there one minute, then not be with us the next. His body was already starting to cool. I touched his beloved cheek, and whispered: "Goodbye, Peter. I loved you so much. I'm so glad you were my brother, and when I see you again on the other side, as one day I'm sure I will, I will give you hell for leaving me."

I tried to smile but I couldn't. I was crying properly now. I let the tears run and so did Val. We sobbed at his bedside, and we hoped he knew, wherever he was now, how much he had been loved.

Once the formalities were over at the hospital and as the reality of Peter's death started to hit us, I was free to return home. The sun was coming up as I drove, and I felt like I was the only driver on the road. The streets all looked the same, but everything was changed.

Opening my trailer door, Diane jolted awake in my armchair. Teddy was lying at her feet, and at the first sound of me, he leapt up and ran to me, his tail going like the clappers, sniffing at me as I petted him.

"Hello, boy, hello," I said, pulling his warm body close to me as he licked the salt tears off my face.

"Oh Barby . . ." Diane said. She knew at once.

I nodded. "He's gone."

"Can I do anything? What do you need?" Diane asked, seeing the grief written all over my face.

"I'm going to walk, with Teddy. I don't know what else I can do."

Diane nodded. "There'll be tea and toast waiting for you when you get back," she told me kindly.

I whistled to Teddy as I walked out and he followed. Hercules nosed around the door of the living room and gave me a sleepy wag of his tail.

"Stay there, Hercules, and the rest of you. Stay. I just need Teddy now."

Hercules slunk back into my bedroom where I heard the snores of the other dogs.

The morning air was chilly but I didn't feel it. We started on a great loop of the site, passing the areas for the dogs, making each one bark in turn, then we headed out to the boundaries. I saw the seagulls waiting for their bread and smiled, envying them their flight, their ability to transcend the plane of the earth and soar into the heavens. Where was Peter now? Would I meet him again? We have a saying at the sanctuary, and among animal lovers, that we will meet our beloved pets, and people, on Rainbow Bridge, and from there we will ascend into heaven, reunited on the other side of this life. The bridge stands between death and rebirth, between the earth and heaven, and all of our animals will greet us on it, sensing our footsteps, their ears twitching, tails quivering, noses catching the first familiar scent of us as we walk slowly, the sun on our faces, delight in our hearts at meeting our beloved creatures and family again.

During the walk, Teddy looked up at me from time to time, as if to ask "Why, Mummy? What's this all about?" yet his face was filled with love and trust.

"At least I have you, Ted," I said at last, long after we'd started to walk, the heavy morning dew feeling cold against my ankles, even though I was wearing my work boots.

I stared at the hillsides leading down to the valley as the sun started to rise, amazed and heartbroken all at once, feeling Peter's spirit soar above the land, up and away from me.

Chapter 18

MEMORIAL

Peter's funeral took place immediately after Christmas; the saddest, bleakest festive season I'd ever known. My brother's dying wish had been to sit in front of my fire and listen to Christmas carols, but I hadn't been able to give that to him. Whether it was an outpouring of grief or a delayed reaction to the hospital banning my attempt to fulfil that wish, I struggled with intense anger and shock in the days after Peter died. I lay in bed each morning, refusing to get up, my eyes sore from a night spent crying.

For the first few days after his death, I awoke to the sound of the cockerels, which, out of the blue had started to crow at the correct time. I had no idea why they had suddenly begun to behave like normal animals, but there it was. There was nothing dafter than the animal kingdom, but instead of getting up and facing the day as I'd always done, I pulled my blankets back over my head and simply lay there, staring at the trailer wall as my tears soaked into my pillow, Teddy by my side.

On the third morning, Diane knocked on my bedroom door. My door was never shut to allow the dogs to come and go, but Diane was being polite, realizing that my emotional state was the reason I was hiding away.

"Room service . . . Sorry to disturb you, Barby, but I wanted to check in and see what do you want me to do with the new cat, Fuzzy? He's just had another epileptic fit and I'm worried the new medication isn't suiting him . . ." Diane paused, waiting for me to respond.

I didn't answer, my face turned to the wall. I hoped Diane, however well meaning, would just leave me alone. I knew Diane was trying to coax me out of my grief by getting my input into the cat's well-being, but the effort involved in leaving the safety of my bed seemed overwhelming.

"Sorry, Di, I don't mean to be rude, but would you please leave me alone?" I said, wiping my eyes.

"I know, dearest, but I need your help with Fuzzy. Do you want me to ring the vet again? He came out yesterday, but I think he needs to come again. . . ."

I ignored my friend, desperately hoping that she'd give up and go away.

"Barby . . . ?" Diane knocked again. It was clear she wasn't going anywhere.

"Alright, alright. I'm coming, wait there," I snapped.

Diane, who seemed completely unaffected by my bad grace, called, "I'll put the kettle on . . ."

I knew this was a ploy to get me out of my bed, to distract me from my misery, to get me to concentrate on the important business of the sanctuary, which never stopped no matter who died or what the world threw at us. The world always kept on turning, a fact which frustrated and soothed me in equal measure. I also knew that things needed to be organized and arranged for Peter's funeral, and even though Val was doing it all, there were still things I could and should have been helping her with.

I pulled on my thick fluffy dressing gown. Bessie, Paddington and Wobbly were already outside, roaming about no doubt, whereas Hercules was sprawled across the rug, and Teddy was lying next to me. He raised his head as I dragged my body out of bed, gently licking my face and the salt left from my tears.

"Get off me, you daft thing," I said, turning my face to him so I could kiss the top of his head. I sat there for a moment, breathing in that smell, which managed to comfort me every time I held my dog close. I stood up, Teddy following me after a big yawn and a stretch. He really was a huge dog now, almost fully grown, standing about thirty-two inches tall. Thanks to the night-light outside, his fear of the dark was no longer an issue, and he used the dog flap confidently each night.

Even though dogs can see better in low light than humans, puppies in particular can experience anxiety overnight, just as young babies do. Dogs have eyes that reflect any light back into the retinas, making their ability to see in the dark superior to that of their humans. Their retinas have more light-sensitive cells, a throwback to their wolf ancestry, along with their sharp sense of smell. Teddy would have displayed the classic signs of being scared when he was left in the dark, tucking his tail between his legs, possibly pacing around, sniffing a lot and even tearing things up as a reaction to feeling scared. I often wondered if he had been destructive in the past because of this fear. His previous owners may not have understood that he was ripping up furniture or upholstery for this simple reason, and it could've been why he was rehomed, though I also had to assume that he had been exposed to dark places while in a frightened state, as he had developed this specific fear.

Whatever Teddy's background, the addition of the bright light outside meant he could live with me for the rest of his days, an arrangement we were both delighted with.

I struggled to remember that delight as I shuffled out to the kitchen.

"I thought you'd never make it," Diane said without looking at me, stirring sugar into the milky tea, just the way I liked it.

I sat down on a chair and yawned. "I'm sorry dearest, I know I'm being sad and cross," I said eventually, sipping my tea. The sweetness gave me an almost instant lift.

"Barby, I know you're grieving, and I'm not trying to suggest you buck up and carry on—far from it, in fact—but I wanted you to know that things do go on, and you will get through this," Diane said, sounding hesitant.

I knew I could be fierce with people at times, so I understood her reluctance to talk straight with me.

"Don't worry, I'm not going to bite your head off. Well, not yet anyway," I said, attempting a watery grin. "I know Peter's dead and there's nothing I can do about it," I added, trying to explain how I felt. "The only thing keeping me going is Teddy. It frightens me when I realize that without Ted, I wouldn't want to go on."

"You mustn't talk like that, Barby. Teddy is a wonderful dog, the best dog in the world, in fact. Yes, we're talking about you, you great lump," Diane said affectionately as Teddy wandered over to her. I watched as she stroked him and whispered loving words into those funny scruffy ears.

"As I was saying, Barby, you're allowed to grieve but I won't let you go under. That's why I'm forcing you up today. It's time to get dressed and do a little work here to stop that happening. The funeral is in a few days so it'll be better to get that all over and done with. You've had the worst news this last week but you must carry on. So many people—and animals—are relying on you." She paused, and I nodded, reluctantly. "Alright, I'll stop now. Meet me in the cattery in half an hour and we'll check Fuzzy out together."

As Diane left, I thanked her. I knew she was looking out for me, and I knew she was right. I had responsibilities; animals and workers who needed me. I couldn't fall apart. It simply wasn't an option.

I sighed, looked out of my window and shivered. It was a cold morning. I didn't have a single Christmas decoration up anywhere though someone had, helpfully, stuck the cards we receive in their hundreds on every surface in the kitchen and lounge.

"I look like I'm living in a card factory, Teddy. Come on then, I might as well get up and dressed or Di won't leave me alone."

In my bedroom I caught sight of myself in the mirror on

my cabinet top. I looked as tired as I felt. I had huge dark circles under my eyes, which were red and swollen from crying. My dark blond hair seemed suddenly to be filled with streaks of gray, and I was sure they hadn't been there a couple of weeks ago.

As a young child I'd learned that life isn't fair, but I had never expected things to turn out as they had. How could Peter, my golden sunny brother, be the one who'd gone first, and at the young age of fifty-eight? It seemed inconceivable, and yet here I was.

I dressed slowly. Teddy was sitting waiting for me. He was still barely more than a puppy, and normally he would have been tearing about the place, knocking things flying, creating the havoc I loved so dearly. Yet despite all his natural instincts for play and fun, he was by my side through some of my darkest days.

Peter's funeral was packed with people, possibly a hundred or more. I'd left Teddy at home with Diane as I hadn't been sure how welcome he'd be in the crematorium. Peter's life was acknowledged and celebrated by his friends and council colleagues. Peter had been responsible for helping to contain the Dutch Elm Disease breakout, which had reached the UK from Europe. He had been in charge of pruning trees with diseased branches, then burning them to avoid the contagion spreading further. His work had been important to the local parks and their ecology, and I'd been proud of him having such a responsible job.

Standing inside the Eastbourne Crematorium in Langney,

surrounded by people who cared for my brother, was an emotional experience. The ceremony was short, as Peter was never one for making a fuss, and we all piled out afterwards into the bitter winter chill. The day passed in a blur. I think I was in shock, and once it was over I didn't go to the wake, preferring to have Ian collect me and head straight back to my familiar zone, the land I turned to in each and every crisis.

Val had announced after the ceremony that a special memorial would be held in Prince's Park, Eastbourne, in spring. A hazel tree would be planted by Peter's colleagues, and we were all welcome to attend. I thought it was a lovely gesture, and I told Val so as I departed.

"Thank you for doing the memorial; I think Peter would've loved the idea of having his own tree. He loved this area, and that park in particular. It's a fitting tribute."

Val squeezed my hand as I spoke. She was close to tears, though she'd been so brave up until that point.

"Dearest, I'm off home. It's all too much for me, and I want to get back to Teddy. He pines for me if I'm not there and it's such a cold day, I don't want him waiting by the gate outside for too long," I said.

"I understand. Yes, you must go, Barby. Thank you for coming, and I hope we'll see you in the spring?" Val nodded.

"Of course, my dear, goodbye."

I turned to see Ian's car parked a little way down the road. I hurried over.

"How was it?" he asked kindly.

"Don't ask," I said. "Let's go home."

Ian nodded and turned the key in the ignition.

We drove home in virtual silence. I tried not to think about the sight of Peter's coffin being pulled back behind the curtain, his body being taken for cremation, yet the sight kept appearing in my thoughts. How could such a vital, lovely man be taken so young? I tussled with my thoughts as we drove, cutting into the silence only minutes from home to enquire about Teddy.

"He's waiting for you by the gate as usual. Don't worry, he's fine. I put a doggie coat on him; we only had one big enough to fit him, and so he's warm enough."

"That's good. I don't like to think of him sitting in the cold," I added.

As we turned into the sanctuary drive, Ian's tires crunching on the gravel, I could see a large black shaggy shape sitting patiently behind the gate post.

"There he is. What a good boy, what a loving dog," I remarked to myself as Ian hopped out to open the gate. My big lump of a dog ran straight through, bypassing him, and headed straight for me.

"You're a sight for sore eyes," I smiled, "but let me get out of this car, you're getting in my way, silly dog . . ."

Teddy was wagging his tail and jumping up in his excitement.

"That's another thing we need to work on," I muttered. "You're too excitable, and some people don't like being leapt upon by a gigantic great lump like you!"

I did love how affectionate and excitable Teddy was, but it was another part of his socializing that I knew I ought to work on. Only a few weeks previously, an elderly friend, a gentleman who walked with a stick, had come to visit and, on seeing me, had waved his stick in greeting.

"Don't wave the stick," I called, but he was too far away to hear me.

Teddy had taken one look at him, and was instantly alert, thinking someone was trying to attack us.

"Don't wave the stick!" I repeated, but my friend carried on, smiling and hollering from the other end of the field. Teddy's nose was quivering, his tail was straight behind him, the muscles in his legs ready to pounce. Then he dashed towards him.

"Put. Down. The. Stick!" I shouted through my hands. At last, my friend seemed to realize what he'd done. Instead of doing the sensible thing and simply throwing it down and standing still so that Teddy could see he wasn't a threat to us, the man's natural instincts took over, and he did the worst thing he could have done: he turned his back on my dog and ran for his life. I'd never seen a man run so fast, especially one who needed to use a stick to get around.

"TEDDY!" I yelled, but my dog ignored me, leaping up at my friend, making him shout. I ran over.

"BAD DOG. Teddy get down!" I called, and at last, Ted listened and pulled back.

He wasn't showing aggression, but he thought this was all a wonderful game of attack and chase, and had frightened the life out of my visitor.

"I'm so sorry, Bill. He didn't understand that you weren't playing. I'd advise never to walk towards us waving anything. To Teddy that's a call to action!"

Later we laughed about it, but I knew I needed to find ways of calming Teddy down. But for now that could wait. Now all I needed from him was a hug and the reassurance that only a dog can bring.

With the death of Peter just before Christmas, I'd chosen not to celebrate it at all. A couple of days before, I'd informed the staff and all my motley crew that I would be working on Christmas morning but after 2 pm my door was shut and no one was to join me. I wanted to hide away with a ready meal and the television. I was grateful that everyone respected my wishes, and when the day came I locked my trailer door and settled down on the sofa with my dogs and the remote control.

Before I did that, however, I made my own small tribute to my brother. I lit a Christmas candle, my only concession to the season, and asked God to look after him until I could see him again. It wasn't so much a prayer as an instruction. The flame bobbed and spun as I made my invocation, and I left it burning on my mantelpiece for the rest of the day, a tiny glowing memorial of my own.

On Boxing Day, I got up and carried on as normal, taking bread to the seagulls at 6 am and then started the business of the day, cleaning out and feeding all of our guests, temporary or permanent.

The rest of winter passed in a bit of a blur, and spring almost came as a surprise, bringing with it new leaves on the trees and the hint of summer days to come. I decided to take

Teddy with me to Peter's tree-planting ceremony, needing the comfort and support of having him by my side.

I watched as Val led the speeches, feeling so proud of her and my brother for attracting so many people to see their wonderful tribute. My sister Pam was there, and we stood together, united in grief and disbelief at losing our beloved brother. I was still grieving, but the changing seasons and the brighter mornings had helped to relieve some of the acute emotional distress I'd felt in the immediate days and weeks after his death.

Many people spoke and shared memories of Peter, and many just stood and listened as the soil was dug and the tree lifted into the hole. Its roots were covered over, and a watering can full of water was emptied over it. The council had built a wooden fence around the tree, and Val had had a plaque made to commemorate Peter and his life. As people started to drift away, I went over to look at it.

I read it through several times. Peter was remembered as a husband, son, father, friend and workmate. There was no mention of him being a brother. I felt devastated. I knew it wouldn't have been a deliberate omission on Val's part, but the thought of being excluded from the permanent memorial brought me close to tears again. Over the years I've had to make my peace with that sign, with Pam and me invisible in the love shown to Peter through that tribute. It hasn't ever sat easily with me, yet I couldn't blame anyone, it was an error not a rejection, yet the thought of it still makes me sad.

Teddy behaved impeccably throughout the afternoon,

sensing my mood and being quiet and well-behaved even in the midst of all the people who attended.

"Perhaps I don't need to train you to calm you down. You must be growing up, Teddy—either that or you can read me like an open book."

Teddy looked up solemnly at the sound of his name. I reached into my pocket and brought out a dog treat, which he crunched on happily.

"Your energy is all used up at playtime with the other dogs, yet you are the most loyal and adoring dog I could ever have.

"When we die, there is a place called Rainbow Bridge that takes us from this life up to heaven. Whichever of us goes first, we'll meet each other there, I promise you, Teddy."

I gazed over at the tree for the last time. I knew I'd never go back there, the plaque's message was too upsetting for me, but I was glad Peter would be remembered to others as well.

"I don't need a plaque to love you, Peter," I whispered, before looking down at my faithful pup.

"Let's go home, Teddy."

Chapter 19

GETTING ON

How I got through the weeks after Peter's ceremony, I don't know. Well, I do. It was Teddy who pulled me through. I believe that a guardian angel was looking out for me when Teddy came back to me after being rejected over and over again, a guardian angel who knew what lay ahead, and sent me this wonderful dog to help me through it all.

Teddy saw me through the immediate terrible grief of losing my beloved brother, and the heartbreak that came with being left off that plaque. As a young girl, I'd always felt invisible, and though I knew it wasn't true, it felt that now—even Peter had overlooked me. This was all nonsense, of course. The plaque was a simple mistake, and it was more an indication of how sad I felt, how emotional over Peter's death, that it became imbued with so much significance.

Life at the sanctuary went on, but for a long time my heart wasn't in it. I went through the motions, preparing for the Summer Fair which was coming around again all too fast, organizing the fundraising, calling the local newspapers to gather their help in advertising our day. I did everything I needed to do, but I know I was still moping. Grief is a strange thing. One day I would feel fine, like I could think of Peter without feeling that my emotions would swallow me whole. Another day I'd be floored by the loss of him, and it would hit me out of the blue, a never-ending tidal force crashing down on top of me again. Teddy was my tower of strength, my constant companion and the creature that meant the most to me during those difficult days.

I still wasn't sleeping, and that contributed to the sense of detachment I experienced during the days as sheer exhaustion left me feeling as if I was swimming underwater most of the time. Each night, the dogs would settle down, the birds in the trees would quieten, the pigs, sheep, horses and goats would huddle together, making soft noises as night fell, yet I lay awake, thinking of Peter and missing my big brother desperately.

Teddy would nuzzle against me, his breathing regular, his hairy body rising and falling as he snoozed, yet always with one ear cocked, as if he was listening for me. Every time I moved, he'd lift his head up as if he was checking I was okay.

"Whatever help I gave you, Ted, you've repaid it a thousand times over," I murmured to him one night. It was a warm June evening. Teddy had been with me for more than a year now, he wasn't a puppy anymore and had a settled routine at night. In the early hours, Teddy would rouse himself, and stretch and yawn before getting up, looking back at me for a moment to check I was still there, and trot out. Tonight I heard the dog flap swing open and once again I felt a huge swell of pride at how far this dog had come, now able to brave the darkness outdoors, thanks to the light of the lamp.

A few moments later, Teddy reappeared, jumping up onto the bed languorously, flopping down beside me, his great weight shifting on the bed to get comfortable.

"Welcome back, lovely boy," I whispered, and got a quick lick on the nose in response.

He sighed a long, contented sigh, and settled down, his head resting on the pillow next to me. I lay there, listening to his breathing as it lengthened and softened, and for the first time in months, I shut my eyes and fell into a dreamless sleep.

"Knock knock, Barby, you're up, that's good," came Ian's voice from the doorway.

"Of course I'm up. What's the matter, what are you bothering me with now?" I asked, a twinkle in my eye.

"Barby, you're back!" Ian exclaimed, grinning at me as he leaned against the kitchen counter.

I knew what he meant. For the past few months I'd gone about my work without a joke or a smile, completely consumed by my grief. Now, having had my first good night's sleep in months, I felt almost human again. It was as if a fog was clearing, and even though I knew it would never go completely, it felt as though I was back in the land of the living.

Not that I would acknowledge this to Ian. He was cocky enough already, I reasoned.

"Enough of your cheek, now, what's happening today? I've

got to call round the traders who give donations of prizes before I do anything. We haven't yet got as many as last year,
and I need to remind them that we need their support."

"Yes, yes, that's all good, but I need to speak to you about
one of the dogs, Billy. I think he's ready to rehome, and I remembered you'd said someone had rung in looking for a dog?"
Ian said, reaching for a slice of my morning toast.

"There's tea in the pot too if you want that as well," I
snapped at him, and he smiled his most infuriating, ingrati-
ating smile as a result.

"I'm going to go out there and tell everyone that Barby's
back, and she's on form, so they'd better watch out," he continued, completely unconcerned by my scowl in response.

Suddenly I laughed out loud. He was right. Something had
shifted, and I felt like the great weight I'd been carrying
around since Peter's death had somehow become less burden-
some, a little lighter, perhaps.

"Well, that's a sound I haven't heard from you in ages,
Barby." Ian chewed his toast and gave me another smile.

"Oh, be off with you," I said, smiling again. It felt good
to feel human again, to feel connected to these people and this
place. I realized at that moment how lost I'd been in grief,
and how grateful I was that the others had taken up the slack
and carried on, doing what needed to be done here, looking
after our animals and overseeing the sanctuary.

"Alright, I'll have a look through my book," I said, picking
up the teapot and pouring us both a cuppa.

In my study, as I called the desk by my armchair, I had a
tatty old black diary filled to the brim with names and num-

bers of people who had rung in to ask about fostering a dog or a cat from us. Every person who had left their number was in that book, but usually I instinctively knew which person would suit which animal. Diane called me the animal–human matchmaker, and she was right. I could generally recall names and faces, and was able to match them up with particular animals. Teddy's case had been very unusual in my being unable to match him up, but perhaps that was because he already had a match in the form of me.

"How's Teddy?" Ian added. He'd polished off one piece of toast and was starting on another, spreading it thickly with soya margarine.

"Oi, you, there won't be enough for my breakfast if you eat all that," I joked. "Teddy is delightful. I don't know what else to say. He's special and I couldn't imagine life without him."

Ian nodded. We all understood how close each other's bonds with our animals were.

I was flicking through my black book when I came across a name.

"This is them, give him a call. I think he'd like Billy, and vice versa. It's good to hear that Billy is better now."

Billy was a Staffordshire Terrier that had been left with us after his homeless owner couldn't afford the vet's bills. The dog had cancer, and we'd been fundraising for his treatment, which ran into thousands of pounds. We'd been unable to contact his original owner after Billy recovered. The mobile phone number he'd given us was out of service, and no one had seen him for months on the streets of nearby Hastings.

We knew it was best that Billy found a new home rather

than staying long term with us as it was his best chance of a normal life again.

"I think it's okay to go ahead and call this person. Billy needs a home and we've tried for months to find his old owner. I'll deal with it if there's any comeback," I said, feeling my feisty old self returning.

I may only be a diminutive woman, but when my temper was roused, I could be a demon, but only where animals were concerned.

"Oh, I know, Barby, he wouldn't dare give you any grief, you're too terrifying."

I gave Ian my best scowl, and at that moment, Teddy came haring in, chased by Wobbly and Paddington.

"Get out you three, there isn't enough room in here for your games," I cried, shooing them back out again. I stood in my doorway, looking at the dogs playing in the paddock, running free as dogs should do. Bessie was trying to keep up, her little corgi legs meaning she was slower than the others. Paddington was rolling over, playing dead, then leaping up and chasing Teddy. Teddy looked like he was grinning widely as he played, darting across the field, his long limbs easily outpacing big old Hercules and poor Bess.

All four dogs looked a picture of health, their fur glossy, except for Teddy's, which was always wiry and sticking up. They were leaping and rolling, running and play-fighting. Every now and then Teddy would growl, or pretend to bite Wobbly, then they'd run off happily, Paddington on their heels, the picture of happy dogs at play.

I breathed in the air. It was that sweet summer smell of

grass and soil. There was a gentle breeze, making the lush green leaves of the nearby beech trees wave at us. As I watched them, sunk in the sanctuary land with its homemade fences, its pigsties acting as kennels, with its mud and chicken wire enclosures, its roughly made goat pens, and my leaky rusty old trailer in the center of it all, I felt my heart swell. My place was here. Peter wasn't with me anymore, but this was his place just as much as mine. That morning I felt him there; I felt his spirit as I watched my dogs play together, as proud a mum as you'll ever find.

Chapter 20

NEW PLANS

After months of forcing myself to engage with the life of the sanctuary again, one morning I woke up to the usual animal sounds and my first thought wasn't of my brother.

"Teddy, Wobbly, Paddington, Bessie and Hercules, I've made a decision," I said, sitting up in bed and making Teddy shift and yawn next to me. "I'm going to build myself a new house."

As soon as I said the words, I realized what an obvious, overdue move this would be. Why hadn't I done this years earlier, instead of just thinking about it?

I looked around the inside of the trailer I'd lived in for more than a decade. It was homely enough with curtains, throws over my bed and cushions, but it was only ever meant to have been a temporary place to live, and it showed. My two saucepans were still in their strategic places, catching the drips from the ceiling. There had been a downpour overnight, and the water was still leaking in. In the lounge I had a further two saucepans of differing sizes in action, stopping the floors getting soaked by the rain. In the kitchen, the window now leaked and I knew without looking that there'd be a puddle of water on the surface.

This was no way to live. It was time to move on, and with my grief on the wane at last, I was starting to feel I had a right to live again, and if that was so, then the first decision I would make would be to build my own house.

"It'll be a bungalow," I said out loud. By now Bessie and Paddington had trotted outside even though it was drizzling. Teddy was still dozing.

"Are you having a lie-in?" I said to him, ruffling his fur on his belly. His face popped up and I stroked his lovely face with two hands.

"We're moving. I'd better tell the others that I'll need to start making plans."

I was up and out before anyone had arrived on the site.

Dad was making himself a cuppa as I crashed into his trailer, Teddy and Wobbly in tow.

"Morning, Dad, how are you?" I asked breezily.

"I'm fine, thank you. You look like you've slept well," he replied, stirring his tea.

Dad was now in his eighties but was still as fit and well as ever. He was a short in stature, like me, with thinning hair and glasses. His eyes still twinkled, though, and he smiled at me as I sat down in his cramped space.

"I've decided that I'm fed up of living in a rusty trailer. It's large but not big enough for me and the dogs. I'm fed up of it leaking and being boiling hot in summer. It's time to move out and make a proper home."

I looked at Dad, who took a sip of his drink before returning my gaze. The bereavement had affected us both very deeply.

"I'm going to ask Arthur to speak to his architect friend. I want to draw up plans for a nice bungalow. It doesn't have to be big, just comfortable enough for me and the dogs, and a big enough lounge for volunteers to drop in and make themselves at home during their break times," I chatted away.

I looked up. Dad's blue eyes were smiling at me, and I felt a rush of feeling for him. He chuckled, which stopped me in my tracks.

"What are you laughing about?" I said in mock outrage. "I'm telling you all about my new plans and you're not listening to a word!"

"Oh, yes I am, it's just lovely to see you look happy again. After our beloved Peter died, I didn't think you'd ever smile again," he said.

"Neither did I for a while," I replied. "For a long time, I trudged through my daily life here. I still did everything I had to do but it just wasn't the same. I felt like none of it mattered, and that scared me. I'd never felt like that before."

"Yet here you are, getting on with your life, making a fresh start. I'm very proud of you, Barby, and not just for that. Look around you—really stop and look around. What you're creating here isn't just a place to dump unwanted animals: it's a sanctuary, a special shelter for animals *and* humans. You have brought people together to care for all the wonderful creatures that are here in your menagerie. It's a remarkable achievement, Barby."

I sat and listened, my cheeks growing red. I never had

learned how to take praise, mostly batting it off and feeling embarrassed, but it meant a lot coming from my dad.

"Thank you," was all I could say. I felt suddenly tearful again, but this time for a good reason.

I got up. Teddy had appeared from outside, and he was far too big to fit inside Dad's space.

"Come on, out, shoo . . ." I said to my dog, smiling. Then I had another idea.

"We're going to go somewhere today, just you and me, Teddy. And I'm afraid we're going to drive there so you'll have to learn to lie down on the seat or the floor. There's no other way."

"Where are you going?" asked Dad, leaning over to give Teddy a pat on the head.

"Just out . . ." I replied, not wanting to explain. I wasn't sure why I was being so mysterious. It was a moment when words failed me. I just had a feeling I knew where I wanted to be.

I whistled to Teddy who was sniffing at something under the trailer and he immediately bounded after me. As I walked, volunteers called or waved and I waved back but kept going. I needed to be somewhere, to put a full stop in place before starting a new chapter in my life.

I put Teddy's lead on, then we made our way through the gate and out of the site. The ground was muddy after the rain and I wore stout boots and a rain mac. We got inside the car, Teddy sat beside me with that funny, lopsided grin of his, refusing to go onto the back seat. His ears were pricked up as he looked around.

"Hold onto your paws, Teddy, we're going on a trip," I said, turning the key in the ignition and starting the car.

I drove for half an hour before reaching the place I wanted to go. I didn't need to gesture to Teddy to get out of the car. As soon as I'd parked, taking care not to stop abruptly at any point in the journey so he wouldn't go flying, he followed me out and onto the pavement.

We walked, me in silence, Teddy stopping every few minutes or so to sniff at new plants or new places along the suburban road. We came to the four large brick columns of the entrance to Prince's Park.

"Do you know where we are going?" I said to Teddy, who had his head up, sniffing the salt of the sea air. Eastbourne's beachfront lay behind us now as we turned into the formal grounds of the thirty-three-acre park. There was a large boating lake which I followed round, knowing exactly where we were heading.

"We've come to see Peter," I said to him.

Teddy looked up at me briefly, but of course my words meant nothing to him. He was following me on the lead, good as gold, and enjoying the new surroundings. The park smelled of that rich scent smell of summer. Although it was edging towards autumn, the storm had served only to sweeten the field and plant life, throwing up the smell of wet grass.

Eventually we got to the field where Peter's tree stood, more than a year older, displaying its light green lushness, the leaves still dripping water from the rain storms.

We came to a halt in front of the fence, which still protected the tree. I ran my hand along the plaque, saying a silent prayer as I moved, willing myself to forgive and forget, and knowing that Peter would never have left me off that thing if he'd been alive.

"I'm told that druids know this as the tree of wisdom and learning. When they make wands, they're made of hazel. Did you know that, Ted?" I smiled. My daft dog was sniffing around the base of the tree, completely ignoring me.

"Peter was a wise man, a gentle soul, and this tree is a perfect resting place for him . . ." I walked around the deciduous tree slowly, its oval-shaped leaves rustling in the sea breeze.

"Peter always loved hazel trees because they provide food for lots of species of caterpillars that become moths, and they provide shelter for nesting birds and the nuts feed the dormice. I bet you didn't know that, beautiful boy."

Teddy turned his big dark soulful eyes to me, but quickly carried on, the new smells were just too enticing.

"They certainly are magical trees," I said, my hair billowing about in the strong breeze.

I stood there for a long time, listening to the tree as the wind blew through it, thinking of my brother in whose name it was dedicated.

"Goodbye, Peter . . ." I said. I had no other words left for him. I'd grieved for many months, but now it was time to start my life again. I wanted a real home, a place that was secure, that didn't leak, that could house my dogs and I in comfort. It was time to start afresh, like the wind blowing off the sea, blowing away the cobwebs of the last year, making me feel alive again.

"Come on, Teddy," I said at last. "Time to go. We've said

goodbye and now we go home." I took a last look at Peter's tree, and turned around, never once looking back.

Once I'd told everyone I wanted to build a bungalow, it seemed that everything sprang into action. Arthur's architect friend did some drawings, and this time, I made sure I submitted a planning application to the council. It would be a modest home, nothing huge or imposing. I wanted a bungalow with one room in the roof for storage, one bedroom, a bathroom, kitchen, office and a lounge—a space where I could look out over the fields of the sanctuary.

The most important thing was the garden. I wanted a proper garden area at long last, not just a few deckchairs in a field. I wanted a small water fountain that tinkled away all year round. I wanted to be able to sit in my kitchen and look out over the valley, drinking in the view inside the safety of my own brick-built home. Gone would be the saucepans on the floor. Gone would be the rickety extension and the trailer steps. I wanted a proper front door and a sun room so I could sit and watch the world go by on the days I wasn't working.

Over the following months, myself, Teddy and the rest of my dogs moved into the tea rooms as the trailer had sprung several new leaks, one of which was directly over my bed. It wasn't the most comfortable arrangement, but it was better than waking up wet each morning.

The work at Pipzedene continued. Every day, there was something new to do, a new animal to care for, a new volunteer to train up, and I felt immense gratitude for the support and love Teddy and I were shown. I know that without my motley crew, my work would be almost impossible. Somehow we all seemed to cope with each crisis as it arose, managing to bring comfort to a hurt, frightened or bewildered animal, and we were rewarded in the trust and healing of those animals. We had 103 cats and 11 dogs in the makeshift kennels. I was already drawing up plans for proper brick-built kennels with runs and accommodation for abandoned dogs. It was becoming clear that we would need to expand, to grow as the need for our help grew daily. The future looked brighter than it had for a long time. As the year drew to a close, and we prepared ourselves for the sad inevitability of yet more abandoned Christmas presents in the form of puppies and kittens, I had a chance to take stock, to look at the last two years and see how proud I was of my beloved hound.

Teddy was a credit to me, to all of us. From a frightened, abandoned puppy, he had grown into a gentle, loving dog, whose only crime had been his size and his deep fear of the dark. As I finished up on Christmas Eve, the second Christmas since Peter had died, I felt that warm glow inside that only the love of a good dog can bring.

"Let's get inside and dream about our new home," I said to him as the sky darkened. I waved goodbye to the last of the volunteers as they left to head home for their Christmas, and turned back towards the tea room. As I walked, I didn't need to look down to know that my faithful dog, the puppy no one wanted, was by my side.

Epilogue

My mission in life is to rescue abandoned, mistreated and abused animals, and if possible, nurture them back to health and happiness before finding many of them new, permanent and loving homes.

In all the years I've been an animal fosterer, I've never had to try so hard to find a home for a dog as as I tried with Teddy. No animal has ever been returned more times, and yet I see it as part of the universal plan. Teddy was meant to be mine and no one else's—it was as simple as that.

Every day I see my staff and volunteers going to and fro, working in the sanctuary. Every day, new animals arrive or are dumped, and they must take them in, no matter how damaged or dirty they are. Our no destruction policy means we aren't selective; we cherish every animal life, no matter how sick or needy.

It isn't easy work. We deal with sorrow as much as joy in our dealings with the shelter animals. Some come in too sick to be saved, others never recover from the beatings or the abuse they suffered.

We try not to judge people but that isn't easy either. Instead, I tell my motley crew to focus on the kindnesses shown by themselves and all the others who support our sanctuary. That is the behavior we must celebrate.

I am deeply indebted to all our friends who have supported the sanctuary, and all the people who give their time to the dozens of jobs that need doing, and all those who work in the community holding jumble sales and coffee mornings to raise money for us.

Listening to the sounds generated by almost six hundred animals on my land as they squawk, meow, bark, crow, bray, grunt and cluck, I know I could never do anything else. My heart is in this land, this special place, made all the more special by the extraordinary people who live and work here alongside me.

Kindness and cruelty are all in a day's work at the Barby Keel Animal Sanctuary, and for many years, it was the love from Teddy, our instinctive bond, the indescribable chemistry between us as owner and pet, which kept me going through all the ups and downs of running such a place. He was a source of immeasurable support and connection.

Teddy had given no indication that he was ill. At the ripe old age of thirteen he was trotting towards me once fine summer day when he stopped suddenly. He looked at me, his beautiful big brown eyes searching for mine when suddenly he collapsed. I think he was dead before he hit the ground. I knelt in the grass holding him to me, his wiry scruffy fur rough against my skin and I wept and wept over his body. Somebody had to pull me off him eventually for the vet to get close.

I had experienced so much grief in my life by then, that for a while, Teddy's death felt like the end for me. I couldn't see how I could go on giving all of myself in my work without him by my side.

When he died, I felt the loss as keenly as that of my brother, of any family member, because I loved him as just that—part of my family and part of my soul.

I had experienced so much grief in my life by then, that for a while, Teddy's death felt like the end for me. I couldn't see how I could go on giving all of myself in my work without him by my side.

No other dog, except perhaps my beloved Gabby, has ever filled that special place in my heart, and I think that now, as a woman in her eighties and still going strong, no dog ever will.

Teddy was special. He and I were connected, and when the day comes for me to pass, I will be running to Rainbow Bridge, scanning the horizon for his scraggy face, his funny sticky-up fur, his black eyes as they twinkle in his grinning face. When he sees me, he'll give a short bark, he'll gallop across that bridge, his tongue lolling out of his mouth, his long limbs scattering everything in his wake. And I'll be there, kneeling in the sweet grass, holding my arms out for his embrace.

Until then, the work of the sanctuary goes on, and the way it does this is with the support of animal lovers, and people like yourselves, the readers of my books. Thank you for buying this. Every penny received for these books goes back into caring for our animals here, and the new ones that arrive damaged and scared, neglected or beaten, to our gates, and into our hearts.

Please help us by buying our books, by donating via our website or Facebook page. We have no PR company, no branding or marketers working for us. We are one of the few remaining private sanctuaries and every coin is used to buy food or equipment to keep the sanctuary afloat and to take care of the vulnerable animals that have no one else to turn to.

I'd also like to thank all the supporters, volunteers and my motley crew, who all bust their guts in their work here, many for the love of it rather than for any pay. They are the beating heart of our community, nurturing animals back to health and happiness wherever they can.